DEVANEY

by Bob Devaney

. . . and friends*

*

Mike Babcock
Don Bryant
Virgil Parker
Randy York

D1383475

Devaney
by Bob Devaney
. . . and friends

Manufactured in the United States of America
First edition
Cover design by Win Mumma
ISBN 0-934904-13-8 (PB)
ISBN 0-934904-14-6 (HB)

Mailing address:
Devaney
5841 Margo Drive
Lincoln, NE 68510

Contents

chapter one

*In 30 years as a head coach
I never had a team
with a losing record*

When making a banquet speech, I often joke about the
very first team I ever coached at Big Beaver High School in
Michigan. I recall that my pre-game pep talk and instruc-
tional speech was always the same. "If we win the toss and
receive the kickoff, let's see who can recover our fumble.
And, if we lose the flip and have to kick off to them, let's
line up quickly and see if we can block their try for the
extra point."

The truth of the matter is that I had two pretty good
teams at Big Beaver. They hadn't won a single game in the
two years before I went there, yet we won eight and tied
three during my two seasons there. I'm very proud of the
fact that in all my years as a head coach — 14 years at the
high school level, five years at Wyoming and 11 seasons at
Nebraska — I was never associated with a single team that
had a losing record.

Not that I didn't make some mistakes during my career.

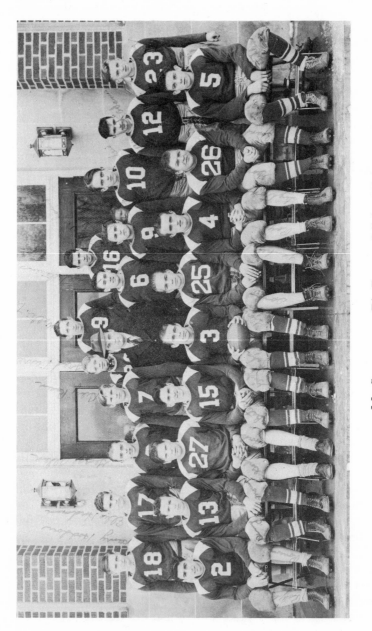

My first team at Big Beaver (Mich.) High.

Probably the biggest disaster I had as a coach was in 1968 at Nebraska. We went down to Oklahoma and got beat, 47-0. We were terrible. That's the game where, when I was leaving the field, I heard some guy calling me a name that sounded something like "Sebastian." I don't think that was the name he meant, however.

That was also the time when I bumped into this little old lady while I was leaving the field. I said to her, "Pardon me, madam, I meant no offense." She said, "Coach, your defense stinks too."

Another fan really got abusive that day. I told him I wasn't going to talk to him because he was drunk. "Yeah," he answered, "but when I sober up I'll be okay again. But, when you wake up tommorrow you'll still be a lousy coach."

The followup on that came the next year. We had to play in Norman again. We got down there and the wind was blowing like crazy. They won the toss and elected to take the wind. Well, they kick the ball out of the end zone. We start at the 20 yard line and run three plays without gaining a thing. Then we punted into that wind and the guy kicked an end-over-ender. The thing bounced back so far the punter fielded it himself on our 18 yard line. We lost two yards on the punt.

On Oklahoma's first play from scrimmage, Jack Mildren ran in for a touchdown. I thought, "Holy mackerel, this is going to be another one of those 47-0 things again."

But our ball club received the next kickoff and went right down the field to score. Van Brownson was playing quarterback instead of Jerry Tagge. Van was the big hero in that game. We ended up beating Oklahoma, 44-14.

Oklahoma still had Steve Owens that year in addition to Mildren. We had a bunch of sophomores.

A lot of people have asked me about that quarterback situation of switching between Brownson and Tagge. Actually, the first two years, when Brownson was healthy, he was probably a better quarterback than Jerry. But Brownson was susceptible to injury. He got hurt in the Colorado

Jerry Tagge (14) and Van Brownson as sophomores in 1969, the year we alternated them so much.

game of his junior year. Then Tagge came in and took over. The senior year was no contest. Tagge was the better of the two.

Van was a good enough quarterback, though. After the '70 season he had a helluva spring. It looked like he was taking over. But then he got hurt again. We took Van to the college-pro all-star game with us as a third quarterback. He got a tryout with the Chicago Bears. But he wasn't a good enough pure passer.

That '69 team, which made the great comeback against Oklahoma on that windy day, had a lot of good sophomores. In addition to Brownson and Tagge, Jeff Kinney was the I-back. Jeff was a very durable I-back all through his career. Of all the I-backs we had, maybe even through those that Tom has had, the most durable was Kinney. He was never hurt. He carried the ball in the 1971 game against Oklahoma on all but one play in that last drive. That was the third-down play when Tagge threw the pass to Rodgers. And we'd have gone for it on fourth down if Johnny hadn't come up with that great diving catch. We weren't going to give up the ball at that stage of the game.

That 1971 game against Oklahoma has to still stand out as the most memorable game of my coaching career. The '69 game was very important, coming back the way we did after a bad start and on the heels of the disaster from the year before. But the '71 game meant a lot more. We were No. 1 in the country and Oklahoma was No. 2. We were playing them down there for all the marbles. It was probably two of the better football teams that ever got on the field at the same time. And beating them, 35-31, on their own field with that last-minute drive, was a great feeling.

One thing from that '71 game that everyone called 'The Game of the Century' really sticks out in my memory — something we shouldn't have done. We had Billy Kosch. And Billy was the fastest of our defensive backs. He was our safety man. But we decided to play him at cornerback and put him on the wide receiver of their wishbone. Well, as a safety man, Kosch hadn't played much man-to-man defense. And this turned out to be a disaster. It made that game a lot closer than it probably should have been.

Mildren was not a great passer. But we made him look like one. We did not play a good defensive game that day. Rich Glover came up with some great plays. But we were a lot better defensive team than we showed. We let them do some things on us they never should have gotten away with. You know, you're afraid you've got to stop Greg Pruitt. But Pruitt didn't hurt us that day. It was their throwing the darn football.

I don't want to blame somebody else, but the plan to put Kosch one-on-one against the wide receiver was Monte Kiffin and Warren Powers' idea. I should have exercised my veto power as head coach and taken a more active role in designing the defense. In certain situations we should have played a zone defense and quit trying to play that split receiver out there man-to-man. That's what Tom now has the team doing against a wishbone. But the wishbone was new then and Monte and Warren felt we needed the support of the safety man against the run. That left the cornerback man-to-man on the wide receiver, and of course that's the greatest passing situation in the world.

Another thing hurt us on defense that day. Mildren was making a lot of big gains on keeper plays. Willie Harper was playing one defensive end for us. His assignment was to go across the line and play the pitch on the option play to keep them from getting the ball to Pruitt. Mildren was making so much ground that Glover wound up going all over the field to make the tackles. So, out of frustration, just before the half, Willie didn't stay out there like he was supposed to. He came in and hit Mildren. And Mildren pitches the ball to Pruitt, who takes off on his only long run of the day.

At halftime I came in the dressing room and Bill Thornton has Willie up against a locker and he's waving a finger in Willie's face and telling him what he's supposed to be doing out there. Thunder was speaking very strongly to him.

Willie Harper, a great defensive end.

Speaking of talking strongly, to digress a moment, I'll never forget the time — I think it was in 1963, just my second year at Nebraska — that Chancellor Hardin brought the King of Tongo Tongo, or some such country, to practice one day. The King has a big turban on his head and colorful long flowing robes. But I didn't see them arrive. People told me later that Hardin was standing there, puffing on his pipe, while the King, with arms folded on his chest, is watching this game called football.

Well, about that time I got mad at some player and yelled, "You ass. Gawd damn, you dumb ass." They say the smoke started to pour out of the chancellor's pipe. And he turned to the King and said, "Your Highness, the coach seems to be rather upset." They left right after that outburst.

We had a variety of people come out from time to time to watch us practice. I remember Jim Nabors and Tennessee Ernie Ford for two. Another was Al Hirt. One time he was in town playing his trumpet at Pershing Auditorium and he came out to watch. Whenever we were in New Orleans I'd stop at his place. He was always very cordial. He put on a great show for our team when we were down at the Sugar Bowl to play Florida after the 1974 season.

But, back to that Oklahoma game of '71 in Norman. We took our own steaks and other food with us to that game. Oklahoma had played a game in Chicago against Northwestern and several of their players contracted food poisoning. We didn't want to take any chances of somebody tinkering with our food. Our trainer, Paul Schneider, tended to get a little excitable before a big game. That's probably how the rumor got started that some gambler was going to poison our food in order to control the outcome of the game. But there was never any basis of fact to that allegation.

We didn't really do anything different in preparation for that game. I hate to say this, but I don't even remember all the buildup and hoopla that went on the week of the game. As the season went along, we had a tendency to shorten practices, not get more intense. We didn't scrimmage or anything like that. Besides, you didn't have to psych anybody up for that game.

I'm getting ahead of myself. I'll come back to that game and all of our games against Oklahoma in more detail later. And I'll take a look at each season and each bowl game we played in and try to analyze them for you. Let's start this story where it began, in Saginaw, Michigan.

chapter two

I wasn't a very big kid
I had to scramble
to make the team

I was born in Saginaw on April 13, 1915. My father, Benjamin, was a sailor on the Great Lakes most of the early part of my life. Later on he worked as an insurance agent and a collector. The last part of his life he worked in a factory.

But I remember him best, while I was growing up, as the first mate on an ore boat. He worked most of the time on ore boats, sometimes on tug boats. My grandfather and my grandfather's brother captained tug boats. My dad worked for them for a while, then he worked for the Pittsburgh Steamship Company on the ore boats.

Because of his work, my father was seldom around during the football or baseball seasons, so he didn't get to see me participate in sports very often when I was in high school. We used to go to the boxing matches together, though. Saginaw was a good fight town.

Grace, my mother, also worked during the Depression when I was a teenager. She made deliveries for doctors. She

Mom and Dad on their 50th wedding anniversary.

Age 2, my parents must have wanted a girl.

picked up glasses and delivered them to the different stores. She also had a job for some time in a cafeteria.

I wasn't very strong as a young kid. I was small. I only weighed about four pounds at birth. I never did learn what the problem was. I was never put in an incubator. They didn't have things like that in those days. My parents told me they didn't know if I was going to make it.

There were three kids in our family. I was the oldest. I had a brother, Art, who was seven years younger than I was. He was an accomplished musician. He was a very good student in high school and got a scholarship to Harvard. He also studied music at the New England Conservatory.

Art wanted to be a concert pianist. But he got in a real bad car accident. It cost him a lot of money, so he had to drop out of college. He was still able to play the piano, so he started playing in orchestras. Probably the best-known dance band he played with was Freddie Martin's orchestra. He played with him at the Coconut Grove in Hollywood for a few of years. Art had his own orchestra at various times in his career. He died in 1968 of an aneurysm in his brain.

My other brother, Ralph, was 11 years younger than I was. When World War II started, he left school to go in the service. He was in the 101st Airborne Division, 506th regiment. He was killed in France, on Omaha Beach in Normandy, during the invasion.

Just as they later did for Art, my parents gave me a chance to take piano and violin lessons. I took piano for about three or four months and violin for about the same length of time. Obviously, I wasn't very suited to be a musician. It was my mother's idea for me to take the music lessons. I also remember my mother helping me a lot with my school work. She was a very smart woman. My father was only home during the winter, when the Great Lakes were frozen over and he couldn't work. My dad died in 1968, the same year Art did. My mother lived in a nursing home later on. She died in 1974.

In Saginaw, when I grew up, there were two public high schools — one on the west side of town and one on the east

A Devaney family outing on the lake. That's Mom holding little brother Ralph, her friend and Dad on the dock. I'm keeping my other brother, Art, afloat.

side. There were also four or five parochial schools. I went
to Arthur Hill High on the west side of town.

Our family home was right across the street from Bliss
Park. I used to spend an awful lot of time in the park, playing whatever game was in season at the time. There were a
lot of other activities connected with the park, and a big
bunch of kids in the neighborhood. So I always had plenty
to keep me busy.

Before getting into high school, where we had organized
teams, we'd just go over to the park and choose up sides for
football, basketball and baseball games. Whatever season it
was. I wasn't much for basketball, although I lettered in
that sport at both the high school and college level.

We'd also play some volleyball with a very crude sort of
net. We were always having some kind of a contest.

They also had boxing matches. It was just sort of a recre-
ational type of thing. But it was very popular. As I said,
Saginaw was a big fight town.

I was a Gene Tunney fan. Also Mickey Walker. And especially Joe Louis. I used to follow boxing pretty close. When
I was a senior at Alma College, I became the school's heavyweight champion. Obviously I grew a lot by then to
qualify for that weight division.

In the first grade, the school I went to was about a mile
from my house. But when I got into the second grade a new
school was built about eight blocks from home. I went
there from the second through the ninth grades.

When I was in junior high, I was still pretty small. I had
to scramble in order to earn a position on every team. I
wasn't an outstanding athlete in junior high at all. By
today's standards I don't suppose I was really very good in
high school, either, although in my senior season of football
I made the all-conference team. I also got an honorable
mention all-state award, but that was about it. When I was
in high school, I still only weighed about 145 pounds. I
played end on the football team, both offense and defense.

Arthur Hill was a big high school. Saginaw, at the time,
was a town of about 80,000 people. Since we just had the

My youngest brother Ralph, who was killed in the invasion at
Normandy during World War II.

two public schools, they had large enrollments. But we didn't have big kids like they do today. The biggest guy on our high school football team weighed only about 200 pounds. I was one of the lightest. Most of the kids weighed about 165 or 170.

I was never serious about anything when I was in school. I got into some trouble with the police when I was in grade school. We broke some windows in the park where we played. The cops raised a little hell with us about that. Even though I wasn't too serious about school, I don't remember getting into much trouble except for that one window-breaking incident.

Saginaw was a foundry town. General Motors was probably the biggest employer. Chevrolet still has a big facility there. The grey iron foundry was, and still is, the biggest in the world. Then there was the big steering gear plant and quite a number of other plants. The main industry in Saginaw was connected with some phase of automobile manufacturing.

I had an uncle, Art Rumbles — Rumbles was my mother's maiden name — who later became executive vice president of the Remington Rand Corporation. He grew up in Saginaw. He was quite a brilliant person. He used to stay with us in the summertime. When he was first married, his wife would come up and stay with her folks. But he'd stay with my folks because he had lived with them before he was married.

Anyway, I used to play a lot of catch with Uncle Art. He was the person who got me interested in sports. But I probably would have become interested in athletics anyway, because in that neighborhood, that's all we did. With the park, we had easy access to where we could play. Sports was the big thing with all of us. We didn't have anything to do with the girls — until later.

I still see some of the guys from that neighborhood once in a while. One is a guy named Fred Graham. Another is Woody Williams. He was a great athlete, but he tore up a knee when he was playing football in high school at Arthur

Hill. He was a super halfback. He could have gone on to be a college star. Woody was also a fine baseball player. But that knee injury ended his athletic career. Graham was also a good athlete. He also played football at Arthur Hill. Another guy was Chet Fobear, a good basketball player and golfer. Then there was the Italian we used to play with. His name was Tony Ellis. We called him Tony the Wop. He was really tough, even though he only had one eye — he lost the other one in a fight when he was 12 years old.

I started following college football because of the older guys I played with who went on to college. I remember when I was young, Red Grange, Benny Friedman and Bennie Oosterbaan were my big heros.

I also followed baseball. I saw Babe Ruth, Ty Cobb and Lou Gehrig play ball. We used to go down to Detroit to watch the ball games three or four times a year.

I played a little basketball. I even coached the sport at the high school level. But basketball was never a big thing with me. Except for the guys who played for the Harlem Globetrotters, I can't remember a basketball player ever being a big sports hero of mine.

The three summers I was in high school I couldn't find a job — because of the depression — so I spent the time bummin'. With a buddy or two, we'd hitchhike or ride a freight train around the country.

A kid named Tommy McFarland and I rode the freights to Florida after we had graduated from high school to try and find some work. We were looking for work in what they called turpentine camps and in the orange groves around the Orlando area. We stayed at the Salvation Army occasionally, but most of the time we just rode the rails and slept in box cars.

After getting down to Florida, we found we couldn't get any work, so we decided to go back as far as Atlanta. We thought it was a nice town and we figured we'd have a good time back there for a few days before returning to Michigan. We didn't have hardly any money. So we jumped on a passenger train behind the coal car. They called that "riding the bumper."

The train was starting up in this little town of Americus, Georgia. But the railroad dicks spotted us. They stopped the train and sent a couple of guys up to kick us off. But we had jumped off and hid in the bushes. As soon as it started up the second time, we jumped on again. But they saw us. We ran up a nearby hill and we hid under a house. It was one of those shacks up on stilts.

These guys came with guns, cops, dogs, everything. They got us out of there, took us down to jail and threw us in. God, we were a couple of pretty scared guys. They said they were going to put us on a chain gang. We were thrown in the same cell with two dudes who had killed a black guy and his wife. They were giggling and laughing. They said, "You two SOBs are in a lot of trouble." That was a hell of an experience for us. When you're down there in that section of the country and in a cell for three days, it becomes serious business. We were in there that long because we had to wait for a guy called the solicitor, a circuit judge, to come around. Fortunately, he let us go. We told him we were down there looking for work and that we were just trying to go back home in the hopes of getting a job in the foundry.

The judge told us not to try to get a ride on a train again or he'd throw the book at us. We walked 14 miles that night before we finally had enough nerve to hit a train again. What else could we do? Without any money, there wasn't any other way for us to get back to Michigan. We looked too bad to hitch-hike.

To compound our troubles, the minute we got back to Saginaw, Tommy and I were right back in jail again. We arrived home the night before the Thanksgiving Day intra-city football game. The east side and west side gangs always met right down in the center of town for a big battle. Tommy and I were part of the west side group. The fight starts and here come the cops to break it up. Tommy and I wind up in jail twice in one week — once in Georgia and once in Saginaw.

That was the only time the cops ever broke up that fight by throwing people in jail. I'd taken part in the battle royal

Arthur Hill High School, Saginaw, Michigan. My senior picture in 1933.

before. But this time we had the traffic all blocked up, so somebody called the police and they loaded us up in the wagon and took us down to the station. The cop who picked me up, hell, I'd played ball with him on the Saginaw police baseball team. His name was Hogan. Man, I was mad at that SOB. But I guess he was just doing his job.

I wound up in jail overnight a few other times in my life. Usually a brawl at a college dance or something like that. Where we lived and worked, people seemed to get involved in stuff like that. There were certain sections of town that were pretty nice. I didn't live in a real bad section of town. It was a middle class section. We had food for our table, even during the height of the Depression. We didn't have many clothes, but we ate okay. We weren't poverty-stricken. We just didn't have any extra money. Once my dad was out of work, we were out of money.

When I got out of high school, the Depression was on. Even though I didn't find any work in Florida, when I got back to Saginaw I got a job in the Chevrolet Iron foundry. The only reason I was able to get a job was because I played for the company baseball team. Jobs were very, very scarce.

My brothers were still in school and my dad was out of work. I was the only member of the family who was employed. I worked day rate at 50 cents an hour. Once in a while I worked on piece work and could make up to $5 a day. That was tops. But most of the time we got a flat $3.50 a day. I'd work five days a week, seven hours a day. So I made $17.50 a week, with a paycheck every other week. I kept two bucks a week for a few beers and my weekend social life. At that time, the two bucks I kept was plenty of spending money. I gave the rest of my wages to my folks. That's what our family lived on.

chapter three

After three years in the foundry
I figured there must be something
better to life than that

After a couple of years in the foundry, because of the Depression, the company curtailed baseball and turned to softball, so I switched to softball. I was a pitcher for the foundry team and played some at second base.

I hated school at the high school level and before. There was too much studying for me. That's why I hadn't given any serious thought about going on to college. I guess I was never really good enough for any university to offer me an athletic scholarship. There weren't many college scholarships in those days. So, when I graduated from high school in 1933, I had to go to work. There was no chance of just taking off and going to college right after high school even if I had wanted to.

I went to work during the day and went out and lived it up at night. That's when I started going out with girls.

My first girl friend was a young lady named Annie Rilko, who also worked at the foundry. She was the first girl I ever went steady with. She worked in the core room, on the assembly line. I worked in another part of the same area. I was 18 years old at the time.

Some of the kids who had gone to Arthur Hill High with me had better situations, but guys like myself, we all had to go out and try to find a job. Quite a few went to work in the foundry. The foundries were integrated. You had white, black, and Mexican. At that time, the foundry was about 30 to 40 percent black, 10 to 15 percent Mexican and the rest white.

The Northeast part of Saginaw was pretty solid black and Mexican. The other parts of town had smatterings. Now the whole town is about 35 percent black or Mexican.

Saginaw probably has about 90,000 population now. I used to get back there when my parents were still living, but now I don't have much reason to go. I was back in 1979 just to visit the cemetery and to see how things were. I visited with a couple of the guys I mentioned earlier.

Anyway, since I never had experienced anything better, I thought I was enjoying my way of life in Saginaw. You'd work or play ball during the day, go out and party at night, then get up the next morning and go back to work. We'd never work on Saturdays or Sundays. So Saturday night was the big time. We really lived it up. There was a gang of guys I went around with, and we'd get involved in things that weren't too great. But we stayed on the right side of the law most of the time. As I look back on it now, we lived a hard life, but had a lot of fun.

After about three years in the foundry, I started looking around and realized I was working alongside a bunch of 50-year-old guys who had been in that foundry since they were out of school. I realized they were still there, doing the kind of work I was doing and making the same lousy 17 bucks a week. I figured there must be something better to life than that. That's when I talked to a guy who I used to ride back and forth to work with occasionally. He was a metallurgist in the foundry. He had been an athlete and had graduated from Alma College, which was located in

The Saginaw Police team. About as close as I ever came to being on the right side of the law.

Alma, Mich., about 40 miles from Saginaw. One time he took me to Alma and introduced me to a coach named Royal Campbell. He had been a coach at Alma College since the days when they played teams like Notre Dame and Michigan State. He was a hell of a coach. Campbell told me, "I can get you an NYA job." I didn't know what the letters stood for — and never asked — but I found out it would pay me $15 a month, and in addition he said they could get me a job waiting on tables or doing some other odd jobs to help me through college.

Coach Campbell was quite a character. He used to sit down, prior to practice, and sip on a little orange gin. He was a very colorful person. But he did all the coaching by himself. He was THE coach and a good one.

In high school, I had two coaches. One was Stan Anderson, who was quite an all-around athlete. The other was a guy named Charlie Grube, also a fine athlete who had been an end at the University of Michigan. Grube probably gained his greatest fame, or lack of fame, when Red Grange ran around his end so many times when Illinois beat Michigan so bad in 1924.

After I had gone to Alma and talked to the coach, I asked my folks what they thought about me quitting my job at the foundry. By this time, my dad had his collection job going pretty good, and he told me that they could get along without the money I'd been bringing in. He told me if I wanted to go to college to go ahead.

I didn't know much about Alma College, or the teams that they played, until I got there. I knew they used to play Michigan State on a regular basis. We played Eastern, Western and Central Michigan when I was there, and all of them are pretty big schools now. Alma played a tougher schedule than they should have, probably. But playing those bigger schools helped bring in some money to sustain the athletic budget and keep the program going. Alma was a church-sponsored school in the Michigan Intercollegiate Athletic Association. All the teams in the league were church-sponsored.

My uncle Art was doing very well at the time. He told me that if I would get some kind of business degree, he would try to find me some work within the Remington Rand Corporation. So when I went to college, I started in business. But I hated that. Most of my courses were business-oriented and my major was economics. But I didn't know much about it. They didn't have a regular physical education course at Alma and they had no coaching courses, so I couldn't go the PE route.

My first years at college were okay. That's when I met Phyllis. She was studying to become a teacher when we met at Alma College. We met one night during my freshman year. She was ahead of me in school, but I was older, having stayed out of school for three years after graduation from high school. We went together that fall and winter and were married that next spring in May. She was a junior, so I went to college for two years after she graduated. During that time she taught in the nearby town of Ithaca.

Phyllis helped me a lot with my school work and was the main reason I stayed in college. I never will forget the one course we took together. I don't think I ever went to class. Phyllis took notes for both of us. Then she wrote both the term papers. And guess what. I got a 'B' in the course and she got a 'C'!

I was actually a pretty good small college player. I made all-conference my senior year and I was captain of the football team and was chosen the Most Valuable Player. In addition to lettering all three years in football, I earned two track letters and one in basketball. I also won the Alma heavyweight boxing title as a senior. Alma didn't have a baseball team, which is why I went out for track. In high school I was a starter on the football, basketball and baseball teams. In fact, I always thought baseball was my best sport. In college, our football record wasn't all that great. One year we had a pretty good ball club, and we were second in the conference; we barely got edged in the championship game. We played Miami of Ohio tough that year. They always had good teams. I played end and linebacker.

I probably couldn't make the Huskers today, but I was captain of
the team and MVP at Alma College.

Alma College. Graduation picture from 1939. Incidentally,
I wasn't the class valedictorian.

We used to play a six-man line on defense, with the ends dropping off the line for pass coverage part of the time.

By the time I was a senior I'd had enough of the business school and economics. I knew there was no way I'd ever become a bookkeeper, and I also knew there was no way I could ever stand to make a living just sitting at a desk. My desire to be a teacher or coach came during the last semester of my senior year, so I talked to Gordon McDonald, who was the Alma coach after Campbell left. McDonald was a great college athlete, and he helped me a lot. But my last year in college was not all that great. As far as the school was concerned, I was not considered their top citizen. I never did anything real bad, but I did enjoy myself. They kicked me out of the teachers college one time because a bunch of us were having a big hearts game. We were also a little inebriated. The dean of women came by. She had red hair, and we hollered, "Hi, Red," out the window. She must have recognized me.

They kicked me out of my teaching classes, so I got myself a practice-teaching job on my own. I was the practice teacher under a coach at St. Louis High School, a couple of miles from Alma. I hitchhiked over there to practice-teach every day.

When I graduated, in June, I started looking around for a job. I spent almost the whole summer trying to find a coaching job — without success. The college didn't help me as far as getting a job at all. I was not an exemplary person in their eyes, so they were not real interested in having me be a representative as a teacher out of Alma College. I knew a Catholic priest who lived in Alma, and late in the summer he told me he had heard about a teaching-coaching job that was opening up at Big Beaver High. That was in August. I figured I wouldn't get the job because school would be starting so soon. I thought I'd probably have to go back and work at the foundry. But I went down to Big Beaver for an interview, and the superintendent, Stuart Baker, needed a guy pretty bad so he hired me.

Big Beaver hadn't won a single football game in the

A budding John Wooden? Hardly. I didn't like basketball, but I coached it at Keego Harbor.

previous two seasons. Well, during the two years I was there we won eight games and tied three. The little town was about 120 miles from Alma, and it was pretty close to Detroit. I don't remember that I even had a teacher's certificate when I got the job at Big Beaver. I guess I must have gotten one, or else they never bothered to check. But I had taken some education courses.

Right up to the time I got the job at Big Beaver, I hadn't given much thought to coaching. As I said, they didn't have PE courses at Alma. So, in my first job at Big Beaver, I just started by teaching the plays we had used in college. I bought some books on coaching and started to study them. Then I went to a couple of clinics to pick up some other ideas.

In that first job at Big Beaver I made $125 a month for nine months. My first year's salary was $1,125. And, in addition to coaching, I taught six different classes. I taught history and eighth grade math and geography among other things. That was awful. I had to go home at night and study like crazy to keep ahead of the kids.

And I coached everything. We didn't have a gym. I had to haul the kids four miles down the road to use another school's gym three nights a week to practice basketball. Obviously, we played all our games on the road.

After two years at Big Beaver I got the job at Keego Harbor. After getting that job, I went back to Alma to talk to my old coach, and he gave me some ideas about a spread formation which I not only used there but was still using some in my final coaching days at Nebraska. That's where you position the quarterback and fullback in their regular spots but use two split ends and two slotbacks. I used that a lot all the rest of my coaching career. In high school I had some plays from short punt formation and even used a little single wing.

I was always trying to improve. I'd talk to more experienced coaches whenever I got the chance, went to clinics and read books. I was always on the lookout for new ideas.

As I said earlier, I joke a lot when making speeches

about my high school coaching days and how bad my first teams at Big Beaver were. I say stuff like, "We lost once in a while. Once a week." Or about the great fullback I had who was 6-foot-5 but weighed only 118 pounds. "The reason he was so great is that being as skinny as he was, he was the only back I had who could get through the holes my line could open up."

They're good stories even if they weren't true. And I'm glad they weren't or I'd have never made it out of the high school ranks. Another story I like is about how dumb my Big Beaver players were supposed to have been. One time I accidentally got 12 men on the field. Our quarterback noticed this dilemma, so he quickly got the team in a huddle and said, "Coach has an extra guy out here, but the ref hasn't seen it. We're going to run an end sweep over by our bench. One of you dumbheads drop out."

The idea was great. There was just one problem. When the team lined up for the next play there were only five guys left out on the field.

When I got the job at Alpena as football coach — where I was for seven years — that's when I first met Jim Ross. He came to Alpena as the basketball coach. He helped me in football and I helped him in basketball. It was a friendship and coaching relationship that has lasted to this day.

chapter four

*I was 41 years old
when I got my first
college head coaching job*

I have often been asked about getting my start in college coaching after 14 years at the high school level. How did Duffy Daugherty know about me? How did our friendship start?

It was when I was the high school coach at Alpena, after my stints at Big Beaver and Keego Harbor, that I had my biggest success in the preps. We won several league and district championships during my seven seasons at Alpena. Michigan State put on spring clinics each year for the high school coaches around the state. It's the same kind of thing we do here at Nebraska. Michigan State would invite in some coaches to lecture. Having had some good teams at Alpena, I was asked to be one of the guest lecturers a couple of different times.

I got to know Duffy then and I think he felt I had some pretty good ideas and that I was able to communicate with the other coaches. Then we had Duffy up to speak at our high school athletic banquet. I got to know him personally.

Alpena High league champs. Jim Ross and I were coaching together even in those days.

And, when I would come down to Michigan State for a game, I'd write Duffy for a ticket.

But I had no illusions about my chances of getting a job at the college level. I was 37 years old. I had made up my mind that if a break didn't come before I was 40, I was going to go back and get my master's degree and take a boring administrative job somewhere.

Then it happened. Biggie Munn was the head coach at Michigan State at the time. Duffy was his No. 1 assistant. Biggie, Duffy, Earle Edwards and a couple of the other Michigan State coaches were over in Europe putting on a football clinic. It was the summer of 1953. They got to discussing their need for an additional assistant coach on the staff. At that time, in addition to the three I've named, Steve Sebo, and John Kobs, who was the baseball coach, made up the staff. Kobs also helped with football and they had Dan Devine as a graduate assistant at the time. He had been a high school coach up in East Jordan, Michigan, and he got to know the Michigan State coaches because they used to come up there about a week before they started fall practice each year and relax for a few days. That was a great area for camping and fishing. Danny got to know them, and they hired him as a graduate assistant.

We had gone on a summer vacation. We were up into Canada. A place called North Bay was our last stop. We had just gotten home. Phyllis and I hadn't been in the house a half an hour when the phone rang. It was Duffy asking me if I'd be interested in coming to Michigan State as an assistant coach. This was toward the end of the summer. They were just back from Europe. I think they had contacted Sonny Grandelius first. But he didn't want to go into coaching yet. He wanted to play some more pro football. Sonny was the fair-haired boy there for a while. So, when Sonny put them off for a year or so — he did join the Michigan State staff later on — they called me.

Maybe I'm wrong about this, but if I hadn't gotten back from my vacation in Canada when I did and they hadn't gotten ahold of me right then and there, they might have

As an assistant to Duffy at Michigan State. That's Houston's Bill Yeoman, second from the right.

called somebody else. I think it was just that close. They
had decided they were going to get another assistant and
they had talked about Sonny and they had talked about
me. I wouldn't be a bit surprised but what they had a third
choice waiting in the wings. I don't know that. But I know
I felt it was fortunate to have been there at the time Duffy
called. When you think about what all that phone call led
to for me at Wyoming and Nebraska, it's kinda scary that
it all came about because of my walking in the door when I
did — and that I might have missed out on the whole thing
if I had been a half an hour later getting back from vacation. But sometimes life is that way. It's often said that opportunity only knocks once. Fortunately I was there when
it knocked.

When the call came from Duffy it was fairly late in the
summer. Practice at Alpena was going to start in less than
a month. It was very awkward for me to go to the superintendent of schools and ask for a release from my contract
on such short notice. I was, and still am, forever grateful to
him for the way he worked it out. His name was Russell
Wilson. The principal of the school was Bill Finch. He had
been a very successful high school coach. He was also very
understanding. Anyway, between Russell Wilson and Bill
Finch, they worked it out.

After seven years at Alpena, both of them appreciated
the fact that I had an opportunity to get into college
coaching — which was very, very difficult for a high school
coach to do. It was also almost a now-or-never situation for
me. I got a late start. I didn't get my first head coaching
job in the college ranks at Wyoming until I was 41 years
old.

If I had gotten started in college coaching as early as
Bear Bryant, or some of those other coaches, I might have
stayed on in coaching longer than I did, hoping I could
break somebody's record for number of wins or whatever. I
might still be trying to hang around coaching. But I knew
that I'd done all I could in coaching after winning back-to-
back national championships at Nebraska in 1970 and '71.

Duffy Daugherty, my closest friend in coaching, the man who recommended me for the Nebraska job.

When I quit I knew there wasn't much else I was going to do in coaching. I had talked to Tom about my job. He had been patient and had waited. Actually, I probably stayed one year longer than I should have as it was. I was hoping to be the only coach to win three straight national championships. I had been in coaching a long time. I was a high school coach for 14 years before I ever started my college career as an assistant.

I liked high school coaching. But it was a great experience going to Michigan State. Biggie and Duffy were extremely close friends. Just like brothers. Duffy was gradually doing more and more of the work for Biggie, organizational wise. After I had been there just one year, Biggie retired as the head coach and became the athletic director. You know that he was thinking about that and had started turning more and more stuff over to Duffy at the time they hired me.

I think maybe it was Duffy's idea to add me to the staff. And Duffy, incidentally, has always been a tremendous help to me. He not only got me on the Michigan State staff to start with, and helped me in many ways while I was in Lansing, but he was instrumental in my getting the head job at Wyoming. And he was in on some phone conversations with Chancellor Hardin of Nebraska — who had been on the faculty at Michigan State before coming to Lincoln — which helped me get invited for an interview for the Nebraska job.

Duffy has been a very good friend of mine all through the years. Unfortunately, I don't get to see him as much as I used to — or would like to. But I have great respect for Duffy. He has a condominium out in Santa Barbara, Calif., overlooking the ocean. He plays golf every day. He lives a good life.

I was also very grateful to Biggie Munn for the chance to get started at the college level. Although Biggie was more standoffish. I never really got to know him very well.

The first year I was at Michigan State we won the right to represent the Big Ten Conference in the Rose Bowl.

Biggie said to me, "You're sure lucky. First year here and you get to go to the Rose Bowl." I said something in jest which didn't help me much. I said, "You guys have been monkeying around for a long time and never could get there. I come in to help out and the very first year we're on our way."

The trip didn't turn out to be that big a deal. Dan Devine, Don Mason and I, as the low men on the totem pole, were treated like second class citizens. We never did get a Rose Bowl watch. Danny felt so bad about being left out that he bought one. And we didn't get to take our kids on the trip with us like the other coaches. Don Mason even had to come out to California with the band. We enjoyed that first bowl trip, but we didn't feel much a part of it.

We made it to the Rose Bowl again two years later. Of course I was a real part of it all by then. We took the kids, got the watches and the whole bit.

Chapter five

*I still like to tell
some of Duffy Daugherty's
favorite stories and jokes*

I first started speaking at high school sports awards banquets and before service club groups and that sort of thing when I was an assistant coach at Michigan State. They'd let us do that to pick up a few bucks. When I was in college I had taken a speech course. I think that helped me some. But the biggest help to me was Duffy. He gave me a lot of tips. I certainly picked up a lot of my ideas from him. Duffy is a great story teller. There are several of his favorite stories that I still tell.

You say to people at a banquet, "You know Charlie here. He used to play golf with Pete all the time. But they don't any more. I asked Charlie how come? He answered with a question of his own. "Would you play golf with a guy who tees the ball up in the rough, gives himself long putts and cheats on the scorecard?" I told him, "No, I guess I wouldn't." And he said, "Well, Pete doesn't want to play with that kind of a guy either."

That was one of Duffy's stories.

Another of his favorite golf stories was about the two guys who were playing behind these two women who were very slow and holding them up on almost every hole. The one guy said, "I'm going up and see if they'll let us play through." But, as soon as he got close enough to see who they were he came running back. The other guy said, "What's wrong?" And the first guy said, "One of those women is my wife and the other is a gal I've been shacking up with." They play a couple of more holes and the second guy says, "Jeez, I can't stand this any longer. I'm going up and talk to them about speeding up a little." So he goes up there, gets a little distance from them and he turns around and comes back. The first guy says, "What's the matter?" And he answers, "It's a small world, isn't it."

Duffy had another good golf story. It was about the golf nut who met this girl in a bar. He was so smitten with her that before the evening was over he asked her to marry him.

"There's one thing you should know about me," he admitted. "I play golf almost every day. And usually 36 holes on Saturdays and Sundays. That could interfere with our relationship, so I think it's only fair that you know about it in advance."

"I appreciate your honesty," she said, "so I think you should know something about me. I'm a hooker."

"Oh, that's no big problem," he said. "If you just move your right hand over a little ..."

Duffy also liked the story about the guy who was in the hospital. He had had his teeth knocked out and his jaw broken in a football game. They had to wire his jaw closed. They couldn't feed him through his mouth, so they gave him some hot chocolate rectally. They put in the tube and poured it in. The guy let out a big moan. The nurse said, "What's wrong? Is it too hot?" The guy mumbled, "No, it's too sweet."

Did you ever hear the poem story? Keats and Shakespeare died the same day and went to heaven. St. Peter met them and said, "What makes you think you have the right to enter?" They said, "Why, we're famous poets."

St. Peter said, "As you know, everyone has to pass a test to enter. If you had told me you were poets, I would have asked you to write me a poem. But, since you claim to be 'famous' poets, I'm going to make it a little tougher. Your poem must include the word, 'Timbuktu.' "

Keats found that no problem whatsoever. He dashed off a little poem quickly and handed it to St. Peter. It read:
"I stood upon the burning sand,
And looked across the barren land.
A caravan came into view,
destination Timbuktu."

St. Peter said, "Very good," and he let Keats into heaven. Then he looked at Shakespeare and said, "How about you?"

Shakespeare seemed a little annoyed at having to go through such a mundane exercise. But he wanted to enter heaven, so in his own particular style he wrote this poem:
"Tim and I a hunting went,
We spied three ladies in a tent.
Since they were three and we were two,
I bucked one and Tim bucked two."

Speaking of heaven, Kansas State football Coach Jim Dickey has a great line: "Everybody wants to go to heaven, but nobody wants to die to get there."

Duffy had one shaggy dog story — those real long, drawn-out jokes — that was also a favorite of his. It was the one about the tailor-made suit.

That's the one about the guy named Freddie who had worked all his life as a coal miner to save enough money for a fine tailor-made suit. He went to the local tailor, whose name was Adam Adamosky, and said, "Adam, I've saved up $400 — my whole life's savings. Can you make me a tailor-made suit for $400?"

Adam said, "My, yes, Freddie. I can make you the finest tailor-made suit in the country for $400." So Adam fitted him out and Freddie came back later and put the suit on. He is walking down the street very proudly and a guy hollers out from the saloon. "Hey, Freddie, I see you got a new suit." "You bet," Freddie answered. "I got it from Adam Adamosky and it's the finest suit money can buy."

The guy says, "It does look like a good suit, but did you notice that the right sleeve of your coat is shorter than the other one?"

So Freddie goes back to the tailor to see about it. Adam says, "Now Freddie, this is nothing to be excited about. This is very high class material. All you need to do is take that coat sleeve in your hand and hold it down. It'll stretch out in no time and be the same length as the other."

So Freddie is walking down the street and another guy stops him. "Freddie, what's wrong with your arm?" Freddie says, "There ain't nothing wrong with my arm. I just got a new tailor-made suit from Adam Adamosky. It's the best suit money can buy. But the right sleeve is short. I'm holding it down so it'll stretch out."

The guy says, "Well, I can see that, but did you notice how the left lapel sticks up?" Freddie looks, and sure enough it does. So back he goes to Adam again.

"I gave you $400 for a tailor-made suit. First, one sleeve is too short and now the lapel sticks up. What are you going to do about this?" And Adam says, "Freddie, this is nothing to get excited about. All you do is put your chin over and hold the lapel down and it'll flatten out. Before long you'll have the best suit money can buy."

So now Freddie is walking down the street holding the sleeve down with one hand and the lapel down with his chin. And another guy saw him and said, "Freddie, what in the hell is wrong with your arm and your neck?"

Freddie answers, "There ain't nothing wrong with my arm or my neck. Adam Adamosky just sold me a fine tailor-made suit. The sleeve is too short and I'm holding it down to stretch it out. And I'm keeping the lapel down with my chin so it'll flatten out."

The guy says, "That's great, but did you notice the crotch of your pants is too long?" Freddie says, "Oh, my gosh, I'm going back again."

This time Freddie tells the tailor, "Adam, I'm getting disgusted with you. The sleeve is too short. The lapel sticks up. Now the crotch of the pants is too long!"

Adam says, "Freddie, if I'd known you were going to be this excitable, I'd have never made you this suit. There's really no problem here. This suit is made with the finest material money can buy. All you have to do is hold up on the crotch with your other hand and before long the material will shrink back up and everything will be fine and you'll have the finest suit money can buy."

Freddie says, "I don't like this, but I guess I'll have to do it." So he walks down the street pulling down on the sleeve with one hand, has his chin over the other way holding down the lapel and he's holding up the crotch of the pants with the other hand.

A couple of strangers are standing on the corner as he goes by. One of them says, "My God, look at that poor old crippled-up fellow." And the other guy answers, "Yeah, but he's sure got a helluva good-looking suit on."

I agree. You should always look for the positive. That reminds me of the time John McKay went duck hunting with Bear Bryant. Bear told him he was the greatest shot in the world. They sat in the blind and a lone duck flew overhead. The Bear took aim, fired and the duck kept right on flying. The Bear was stunned. "John," he said, "you are witnessing a miracle. There flies a dead duck."

My favorite fishing story is about George, who was the envy of every fisherman in the area. He always came back with a boatload of fish. The game warden got suspicious, so one day he asked George if he could go along. So George took him out in the boat. When they got out in the middle of the lake, George took out a stick of dynamite, lights it and throws it out into the lake. BOOM! A whole bunch of dead fish come up to the surface. George scoops up the fish into the boat. The next thing he does is light another stick of dynamite. He hands it to the game warden and says, "Are you going to just sit there and look at it or are you going to fish?"

When I was coaching at Wyoming, I visited the prison at Rawlins one day. I saw this very distinguished looking grey-haired gentleman. I told him he certainly didn't look like the "criminal type." I asked him what he was in for? "Well," he said, "I was accused of rape." I asked him if he did it? "No," he answered, "but the evidence was so flattering I pleaded guilty."

Then there was the time I was standing on a corner next to this blind man with his seeing-eye dog. The light turns red, but the dog starts across the street with the man anyway. The horns honk, brakes are squealing. Miraculously, they get to the other side. The blind man reached in his pocket and pulled out a piece of candy for the dog.

About that time I got over there and said to him, "Gee, this dog almost got you killed, bringing you across the street against the red light, yet you are about to give him a piece of candy." The blind man said, "I'm just trying to find out where his head is so I can kick him in the ass."

While I was coaching at Big Beaver High, the little town stayed exactly the same size all the years I was there. I asked the guy from the Chamber of Commerce how come. He told me, "It seems like every time a new baby is born, some guy leaves town."

While I was coaching, I did a lot of research on the history of sports. I looked into the role that the yell leaders play in front of the crowds. I found out that the first yell was, "Hooray for our side!" It was initiated in England when Lady Godiva rode side-saddle down the streets of Coventry.

Some people say that in sports, winning is everything. Well, I don't know about that. You take Eddie Fisher for example. He was married and divorced by Debbie Reynolds, Elizabeth Taylor and Connie Stevens. Now there is a guy who had more fun losing than most of us do winning.

Duffy never worried about winning. He had a special play to cover all occasions. At the end of every game, win or lose, he had two of his biggest linemen lift him to their shoulders and carry him off the field. He figured the people in the stands would always say: "Look, there goes good old Duffy again. He might not be much of a coach, but his players sure love him."

Duffy's wife was very understanding after an important game. When he'd get home, she always had his robe, slippers and hot water waiting for him. She didn't like him washing the dishes in cold water.

In 1965, when Michigan State finished 10-0, a reporter asked Duffy if it was his finest season. Duffy said: "You could say it's one of the best starts we've had in recent years." When he went 3-7 in '67, Duffy said Michigan State won three games, lost none and was upset in seven.

One of my favorite stories didn't come from Duffy. It's about the Jewish man who goes into a bar and sits down next to this good-looking girl. She says, "Would you like to have a drink?" He says, "Vell, I'm no Dean Martin, but I vill take a drink."

After they have the drink, she says, "I'd like to take you out to dinner." "Vell," he says, "I'm no Duncan Hines, but I do appreciate good food." So they go out to dinner.

After dinner she says, "Would you like to go to the concert? I have some tickets." "Vell," he says, "I'm no Dave Brubeck, but I do appreciate good music." So, they went to the concert.

After the concert she says, "Would you like to come up to my apartment?" "Vell," he says, "I'm no Errol Flynn, but I do appreciate good company." So they go to her apartment.

The next morning they get up and she says, "Now I've wined you, I've dined you, and I've entertained you. How about some money?"

"Vell," he says, "I'm no gigolo, but I vill take twenty dollars."

chapter six

*So I said
if he stays,
we all stay*

On Thanksgiving Day in 1957, my first season of coaching at Wyoming, we played Denver University in Denver and lost a tough ball game, 14-13. Denver was Wyoming's most bitter football rival at the time. The game was on regional television, as I remember, and we were all pretty down and out about the loss. It was a custom at Thanksgiving for the Wyoming team to stay in Denver the night after the game, even though we easily could have returned to Laramie. Phyllis and I and Jim Ross and his wife, Maurine, had been out to eat, and we had just come back to the hotel. I was up in my room when an official from the hotel knocked on the door and said a couple of our football players was in trouble downstairs in the lobby.

I went down and found two of our players, a big Polish kid from northern Wyoming, and a real tough Italian from New Jersey, with our backfield coach Mike Corgan, who was wearing a T-shirt and standing in the hallway with a policeman and the house detective. The house detective didn't have any sleeve on his coat. What had happened was, they had gotten into an argument before I got down there, and when the house detective tried to grab Mike, Mike ripped the sleeve off his coat. It seemed that the two kids were coming into the hotel, and they might have had a few drinks, when the house detective stopped them and asked to see some identification. We were all staying there, we were guests, remember, and this house detective challenged them and wanted to search them, for what, I don't know. The players were madder than hell because they were guests. When the guy tried to search them, that's when the hassle started.

Everything might have been calmed down a little bit except that one of the cops pointed at the Italian and said he was going to take him down to the jail. He grabbed the kid, and the kid just picked him up by the front of his uniform and threw him right on his back. Slam, right on the floor of the lobby. The policeman jumped up, with his gun in his hand, and fired a shot that went up through the rooms upstairs. Fortunately, no one was hurt, but we said, "Okay. We'll go along with you." What else could we do? The guy was hysterical, and he was waving his gun around. So the two players, Mike Corgan and myself got in a police wagon, went down to the station, and sat around for awhile. The night officer at the police station was a little more calm than the cop with the gun, and it looked like everything was going to be all right. But the one hysterical cop kept bitching about the incident, pointing at the Italian who had thrown him on the floor, and saying: "Well, the rest of these guys can go, but this one's staying."

By then I thought we had things well enough in hand, what with the calm policeman and my being a head football coach, that I pressed my luck and said, "Well, if our player stays, we all stay." So we did. First, they tossed us in the drunk tank and then, for some reason, they put us in a cell by ourselves. Since Mike was wearing his T-shirt, Jim Ross had to come down with a regular shirt so Mike would have something decent to put on before we went to court in the morning. We were brought to trial, and they declared the Polish kid and me innocent. They dismissed Mike, I think, or gave him a suspended sentence, and they gave the Italian kid a suspended sentence.

We got a lot of publicity about the trial. I was on a recruiting trip a week or so later in Nashville, Tennessee, and a bellhop said: "Hey, I recognize you. I saw your picture in the paper." Really, it was just an unfortunate incident. When the Laramie newspaper reporters asked the president of Wyoming University, Dr. Duke Humphrey, if he was going to fire us, he said: "Hell no." Just like that. He said we were just sticking up for our players, so why should he fire us. Duke was a character himself. People used to ask him if there were any exceptions to the university's entrance requirements, and he'd say: "You bet, for anybody who's a good football player." Bowden Wyatt described Duke Humphrey better than anyone else ever could. He said Duke looked like a streetcar conductor who had lost his hat. But, Bowden added: "Never underestimate the guy."

Bowden helped me get the Wyoming job. Bowden and Duffy. They both called Red Jacoby, who was the Wyoming athletic director, when Phil Dickens decided to leave for Indiana after his 1956 Wyoming team went undefeated at 10-0. Red thought the sun rose and set on Bowden Wyatt, who was a coaching legend at Wyoming before Dickens, and he knew Duffy Daugherty, too. Duffy and I met Wyatt in a clinic at Michigan State when I was still an assistant coach there and Wyatt was turning out some good teams at Tennessee.

I had never thought much about taking the job at Wyoming. I thought I was going to get the head coaching job at Missouri when Don Faurot retired as the coach after the 1956 season. They promised me the job at Missouri, in fact.

Don was the athletic director, and he said: "The job's yours. Just go home, get your staff organized, and we'll call you." I started asking people about going down to Columbia with me, and I never heard from Faurot again, so I called him. He said, "Oh, there's nothing to worry about; just get your staff together." I didn't hear from him again, and when I called him the next time, he said: "I've got some bad news for you, Bob." I don't know if Don had much say in the matter, but they hired Frank Broyles as their new head coach. Frank coached at Missouri one year, then he left for Arkansas, and they hired Danny Devine, who had coached on the Michigan State staff for Duffy, too.

I knew the Wyoming job probably wasn't quite as good a job as the one at Missouri, but I didn't like Columbia. I mean, I didn't like the town at all. I didn't like anything about it. To me, it was just such a contrast to where I came from and where I had lived all my life. People were stilted in Columbia. They didn't seem like the kind of people I liked to be around. At Wyoming, everyone was friendly.

I learned to love Wyoming.

I suppose going to Wyoming instead of Missouri was a little bit of a comedown, but I wanted to get a head coaching job. I also had a chance to go to Colgate about that time. I went for a visit, but I could tell the atmosphere was a lot different. They wanted to win at Wyoming. At Colgate, well, I'm not too sure. They weren't involved in a situation that was conducive to winning. In Wyoming, being away from all the population centers, recruiting was a problem. You were aware of that when you went there; you could tell right away that recruiting was going to be a key factor, but they had good facilities, and I was impressed that they wanted to have a football team. As a result, we had plenty of financial backing. At that time, that area was getting a lot of money for oil rights. We didn't have an alumni association, but we had enough money to run things ourselves. We never had an alumni meeting

My first staff at Wyoming, which included Melton, Ross and Corgan.

when I was at Wyoming, in fact. Never. One of the administrators said: "We don't want to mess with one." The athletic department had one old rich guy who used to give it about $10,000 a year. It wasn't like Colgate, and, like I said, I needed a head coaching job.

For my first coaching staff at Wyoming, I got Lloyd Eaton from Northern Michigan. He was the head coach there, but he decided to come to Wyoming with us. John Tobin had been an assistant coach at Hillsdale College in Michigan, and Jim Ross was still coaching at Alpena. Mike Corgan had been a high school coach for 15 years in Michigan, the last five of those years at Muskegon Central Catholic. I remember one of my teams at Alpena beat one of Mike's Petosky teams 33-14. I don't think he's ever forgotten that one. Also, we wanted to get a couple of guys on the staff who were familiar names among Wyoming high school coaches, so we asked Red Jaboby which coaches had the best records there, and he said Carl Selmer and John Melton. Red didn't hesitate. There were other guys with good coaching records at smaller high schools, he said, but those two were the best, and what made it even better was, they had both played at Wyoming. Carl hadn't been a real good player, but John was a pretty good fullback for a Wyoming team that went to the Gator Bowl in 1951 and beat William and Mary. Carl had been coaching at Worland, Wyoming, for nine or 10 years and hadn't lost many games, so we went up to Worland and talked to him about coming down to Laramie with us. We wanted John, too; he'd been coaching at Thermopolis, Wyoming. I looked up his record there. John's teams were 47-13. We needed a dormitory director, so he and his wife, Bev, ran the athletic dorms for us. John was the assistant freshman coach then. Carl was the head freshman coach; Lloyd Eaton coached the defensive line; Jim Ross had the defensive backs; John Tobin handled the offensive line; and Mike Corgan was our offensive backfield coach. It was a good staff.

We won our first game, 12-7, over Kansas State and finished 4-3-3 in our first season. We had the best overall defense in the Skyline Conference and led the conference in defense against the rush.

Laramie was an interesting town. It had an Elks Lodge downtown, where there were some slot machines, and coaches would go down there every night after practice. On Saturday nights there would be a dance band at the Elks, and we'd take the wives. When it got warm enough and we could find someplace to play, we'd play a little golf here and there. I liked Laramie a lot.

We had some real dead-end kids on those first Wyoming teams. We had one quarterback who transferred there from a "college" in Michigan, Ionia Reformatory. We didn't know it at the time, but this kid had been convicted and imprisoned twice for armed robbery. The kid's parole officer was a friend of Jim Ross and he contacted us about giving the guy a shot at playing football at Wyoming. We didn't know all about his background, but we met him and he was a fine-looking young man so we decided to give him a chance and offer him a scholarship.

This was in 1957, when we were still getting settled, and Mike Corgan had a car he wanted to get out to Wyoming. Since this quarterback was coming out, Mike decided to let him bring the car when he came. It had a bunch of plants in it . . . you know how Mike likes to grow plants; he's always had that green thumb. Well, the quarterback, the car and the plants didn't show up for more than a week, and we couldn't figure out what had happened. I think Mike was more concerned about his plants than the car. Finally, the guy showed up, and he looked like he'd lost 10 or 12 pounds. He was a ragged-looking guy by the time he got to Laramie. He said he'd stopped off in Chicago for a few days, but he didn't say why. Mike's plants were all dead, of course.

The kid might not have been too reliable as a cross-country driver, but he wasn't a bad quarterback. The only problem was, he drank some and we could never catch him at it. We couldn't even figure out where he was hiding the stuff.

He'd come out to practice, and we'd know damn well he'd had something to drink. We also thought he was stealing things out of dorms, but we couldn't prove that, either. In 1958, he started against the Air Force, and we played him the whole game. Air Force had one of its best teams ever. Ben Martin was the coach; they had a quarterback named Rich Mayo; and they played in the Cotton Bowl that year. This quarterback of ours nearly beat them. We lost in the last quarter, 21-6.

So anyway, this quarterback ... we finally found out about his drinking. There were vines on the side of the athletic dorm where he lived, and he'd put a string around his bottles, tie the string to the vines, and let the bottles down into the greenery so we couldn't find them. We finally found out, or maybe he told us, when he left school. He'd just pull the bottles up when he wanted them and let them back down when he was finished. I think he probably drank about anything he could get ahold of.

Finally, he'd been in so much trouble, we kicked him off the team and almost ran him out of town. He did something one day, I don't remember what, and Mike Corgan told him to get out. Mike said: "I'll take you down to the bus station." Before they could go to the bus station, though, they had to go find some bottles of whiskey this guy had stolen from a Laramie hotel where he tended bar for awhile. The owner said he wouldn't prosecute if he got the whiskey back, so he and the kid and Mike went to look for it. The kid said he'd hidden the whiskey in the cemetery not too far from campus. The two of them drove out there, and the kid started looking around. Mike was madder than hell because he was looking behind tombstones, and all of a sudden, the kid said: "Oh, I betcha I know what happened to it. When I was hiding the whiskey, there was a priest over there watching me, and I bet when I left, he took the whiskey." Mike's a good Catholic, and he jumped about a foot in the air when he heard that. He said: "Get in the car. You've had it!"

Instead of going right to the bus station, though, they

drove back to the dorm because the kid said he wanted to say good-bye to a few of his friends. Then he said he had to sell a lamp he couldn't take with him on the bus. He took it down to a guy's room, and the guy said: "Hey, that's my lamp." He was trying to sell a stolen lamp. Mike finally got him in the car and headed for the bus station. They stopped a couple of places on the way, and by the time they got to the station, the quarterback was so drunk he could hardly stand up. Each time he stopped to tell someone good-bye, Mike would watch him go in and come back out, but he must have gotten a drink or two inside because he'd had so many drinks when they arrived downtown that he was drunker than hell.

We had another character who later became a professional wrestler; he may still be wrestling somewhere. When he came out to Wyoming, he was on probation for something. I think he was from Massachusetts. He transferred to Wyoming from Notre Dame. We called a Notre Dame assistant coach who said he was a fine kid but that he'd had a little problem with his grades and thought it would be better for him if he transferred and got a new start. I'll bet he raised as much hell there as he did when he got to Laramie. He was bad all right. He played several years in the Canadian Football League, and I remember his team up there had a retirement banquet, an honorary deal for former players, and when he was introduced, you could hardly hear any applause. They said his teammates used to boo him when he came into the locker room. He played in Canada for five or six years and then he became a professional wrestler. He was huge.

We sent him a first-class airline ticket so he could make a recruiting visit to Wyoming. He cashed in the ticket and brought his wife along, which was somewhat illegal since it was supposed to be his official visit. He got there and then stayed, which I think also was somewhat illegal. We were put on probation for one year by the NCAA.

Anyway, this kid from Massachusetts, he was mean even

when he was scrimmaging against his own teammates. He'd come across the field and make cut-off blocks, clip people, stuff like that. The guys all hated him. When he wasn't scrimmaging, he used to squat down by the fence along the sideline and hang onto it. One day somebody said, "Look, they got him chained to the fence." Naturally, he didn't hear that remark.

He never played for us; he got kicked out of school before he was eligible to play.

chapter seven

*We can't get out
on this side;
there's water here*

Carl Selmer and I drove a University of Wyoming car up to Douglas, Wyoming, one day to be guest speakers at a Boys State meeting. We didn't leave Douglas to start back to Laramie until late in the day. It was tough getting to and from Douglas, because it was in an out-of-the-way location, and the two-lane road we had to take just south of Glendo was narrow and winding. We were both pretty tired. I was driving, and not too far down the road from Glendo, around Wheatland Pass, I missed a turn.

I was sleepy and I guess I wasn't handling the curves too well, but as soon as we went over the edge and started down the embankment, I was wide awake. I tried to hold the steering wheel steady as we bounced along, and I thought I'd done a pretty good job of driving that son-of-a-gun down the hill, but when we stopped, right in the middle of a trout stream, Carl was on the driver's side. We were both pretty dazed from the accident, and we didn't think much about it at the time; we were just glad to be alive. But I still don't know how he got over to the driver's seat because I'm certain he was on the passenger's side when we left the road. I guess the car had rolled over a few times. Anyway, Carl opened his door and started to get out, but he pulled back in and said, "Bob, we can't get out on this side; there's water here."

Neither one of us was thinking too clearly. We left the car in the trout stream and climbed back up the hill; it was pretty steep, and we were worn out by the time we got to the top. We walked down the road in the direction of a light, which turned out to be in a cabin. We knocked on the door, and an old guy answered after a couple of minutes. He had a whole table full of empty beer bottles, and there were empties scattered all over the floor. Apparently, he'd been sitting there with nothing to do but drink beer. There was no telling how long he'd been at it, but we didn't have to be too alert to know he was drunk.

We said we had run our car over the hill when a deer ran across the road, and we needed to use his telephone. He said he didn't have a phone, so we asked if we could get a ride up to the corner where we could at least hitchhike. We were pretty messed up from the accident, and he looked at us and said, "Geez, you guys look like you're drunk." Can you imagine that, him telling us we looked drunk when he had those empty beer bottles all over the place? Anyway, after awhile, we talked him into giving us a ride to the corner, and we finally reached a phone and called Phyllis. She came and picked us up, 14 or 15 miles outside of Laramie.

When we got back to Laramie, we told a guy from the university motor pool about nearly missing a deer and where we had left the school's car. He sent someone out with a wrecker to pick it up. The problem was, he couldn't find the darn thing. It was so far down the hill away from the road — it must have been a half a block or even three-quarters of a block down — you couldn't see it, and he had a heck of a time, so he gave up looking for it and came back. Carl and I had to go along and show him where the

Now you can see why the Sun Bowl game wasn't played
in Laramie in 1958.

car was. It wasn't in very good shape, the roof was badly dented, and we had a tough time getting it back up the embankment. Fortunately, no one asked any embarrassing questions about how we had driven off the road. We were lucky to get out alive; we might have been killed. I'll tell you, that was a dandy.

Our making up the story about the deer running across the road reminds me of a little story I used to tell when I spoke at high school athletic banquets not too long after I came to Nebraska. It went like this.

Tony Jeter, Freeman White and Monte Kiffin all went to a party one night during the football season and missed curfew. We didn't have a lot of rules, but an 11 o'clock curfew was one and I had to enforce it, so I called those three players into my office, one at a time, to see if their stories fit. While the other two waited outside, Jeter came in first. I said, "Tony, I understand you missed curfew last night, and I'm going to give you a chance to admit it before I decide on the proper punishment. What do you have to say for yourself?"

Tony said: "Well Coach, I admit I was late, but you see I was at this party on a farm, and when I noticed it was getting close to 11 o'clock, I tried to call a taxi. I couldn't get a cab, so I started walking to town. About halfway back, a farmer came by in a wagon pulled by a horse and offered me a ride. I got on, and we were almost back when the horse stepped in a hole and broke his leg. The farmer had to shoot the horse, and I had to walk the rest of the way. By the time I got home, it was past the curfew."

I sent Tony out and called Freeman White into my office. I said: "Freeman, I understand you missed curfew last night, and I'm going to give you a chance to admit it before I decide on the proper punishment. What do you have to say for yourself?"

Freeman said: "Coach, I admit I was late, but you see I was at this party on a farm, and when I noticed it was getting close to 11 o'clock, I tried to call a taxi. I couldn't get a cab, so I started walking to town. About halfway back, a farmer came by in a wagon pulled by a horse and offered me a ride. I got on, and we were almost back when the horse stepped in a hole and broke his leg. The farmer had to shoot the horse, and I had to walk the rest of the way. By the time I got home, it was past the curfew."

Well, I sent Freeman out and called Monte Kiffin into my office. I was getting a little suspicious by then, but I said: "Monte, I understand you missed curfew last night, and I'm going to give you a chance to admit it before I decide on the proper punishment. What do you have to say for yourself?"

Monte started right in on his story: "Coach, I admit I was late, but you see I was at this party on a farm, and when I noticed it was getting close to 11 o'clock, I tried to call a taxi."

At that point, I stopped him. "Now wait just a minute, Monte," I said. "Let me tell you the rest. You couldn't get a cab, so you started walking to town, right? About half-way back, a farmer came by in a wagon pulled by a horse and offered you a ride, right? You got on and were almost back when the horse stepped in a hole and broke his leg. The farmer had to shoot the horse, and you had to walk the rest of the way. Is that what happened?

"Well," Monte said. "That's not quite right, Coach. A farmer did come by in a wagon pulled by a horse and he did offer me a ride. I got on, but when we got to the edge of town, we had to stop. We couldn't go any farther because there were two dead horses in the middle of the road."

Of course, that didn't happen, but Monte was the kind of guy who could have made up an excuse like that.

Carl Selmer wasn't the only assistant coach with whom I ended up driving into a ditch in a university automobile. John Melton, Red Jacoby, who was the Wyoming athletic director, and I had a similar experience one time when we went to Kemmerer, Wyoming, out in the western part of the state. As I recall, it happened not too long before I took the job at Nebraska.

We spent the evening at a piano bar in Kemmerer, listening to Red Nichols and the Five Pennies. I'm not sure whether we stayed there all night or went on north to Jackson, but anyway, the next day we had to get to Casper, which was a long drive, almost clear across the state. John was driving, and he and Red got in an argument about something, I don't recall exactly what. About the time Red told John, "Anybody who would say something like that, shouldn't be working for me," John drove the damn car in the ditch. He must have been paying more attention to Red and the argument than he was to the road.

Well, there we sat, in the ditch, and finally, Red told John he'd have to walk somewhere to try to get some help since he was the one who drove the car in the ditch. So John took off walking down the road to find help. While he was gone, we started screwing around with the car, and we managed to back it up and drive it out. It wasn't very steep in between roads. We picked up John going down the road, and as soon as he got in the car, John said he hoped we'd take the job at Nebraska because Red was going to fire him anyway.

chapter eight

*If you come here
and win, you'll
never be sorry*

We couldn't waste any time after we got to Wyoming.
We no sooner had arrived in Laramie and got located than
everyone wanted to know when we were going to start
spring practice. The Wyoming fans were itchy after the 10-
0 record the year before. Wyoming had an indoor arena
where they held rodeos and could put down a basketball
floor during the winter when they weren't practicing football. The footing was pretty good in there, so we started
spring practice about the first of February. I don't think we
got done until the end of April.

Our first team at Wyoming went 4-3-3, despite all of
those indoor practices. Our second team went 7-3 and then
beat Hardin-Simmons, 14-6, in the 1958 Sun Bowl game,
but we had one heck of a football team, probably our best
at Wyoming, in 1959, finishing 9-1. We would have gone to
a bowl game that year, too, but we were on a one-year
probation, which made us ineligible under NCAA regula-

tions to compete in any post-season games. As I've mentioned before, the previous year, a guy who had talked to us about transferring schools came out on what was supposed to be a recruiting visit and just stayed, which was a violation. The rule stated that a school could pay for a recruit's transportation on his official visit but that visit couldn't last more than 48 hours. When the guy stayed, it wasn't a visit, so we were considered guilty of paying a player's transportation to school. That was illegal. To make it worse, the guy had cashed in the first-class airplane ticket we sent him and used the money to bring his wife. He never played a down of football for Wyoming, but he probably cost us a bowl bid.

Our line in 1959 was very good and it averaged only 191 pounds a man. Our backfield averaged maybe that much, too. When we came to Nebraska and saw all those bigger kids, guys like Bob Brown and Lloyd Voss, we were afraid they wouldn't be quick enough. We felt they just wouldn't be able to move like the smaller players we had at Wyoming. We came to find out later that they could move pretty well.

The only game we lost in 1959 was to Air Force, in Laramie. We didn't play a very good game that day, and they beat us 20-7. We won most of our other games by big scores; we just beat the heck out of some teams. In the first game of the season, in Billings, we beat Montana 58-0. We beat Denver 45-0 and Colorado State 29-0. Except for Air Force and New Mexico, no team scored more than seven points against us.

We went out to North Carolina State and beat them 26-0 in their homecoming game. Earle Edwards, who had been an assistant coach at Michigan State when I was there, was North Carolina State's head coach and Roman Gabriel was the quarterback, but he was hurt and didn't play; he became an All-American and later played for the Los Angeles Rams. He did play against us the next year. He was a great passer, but our defense handled him real well and we beat 'em.

Anyway, that 1959 game was one week before John Tobin, our offensive line coach, died of a heart attack. John suffered it during a game against Utah. He was in the press box when he had the attack, and they rushed him to the hospital. We went to the hospital after the game and were all kidding around with him. We left, and about an hour later the hospital called to say John had died. I had to tell John's wife; that was tough. After John died, we switched Carl Selmer from head freshman coach to coaching the offensive line.

We played New Mexico in the next-to-last game of the year — Denver came later, at Thanksgiving — in Albuquerque. Our last five games all were on the road. In fact, we never played more than four home games in a season while I was there, and we never played a home game after the middle of October because it was too cold and windy in Laramie. Marv Levy, who coached in the Canadian League before going to the Kansas City Chiefs, was in what turned out to be his final year of coaching at New Mexico, and he had an All-American running back named Don Perkins, who became a star for the Dallas Cowboys. Both teams had 7-1 records, and we had one heck of a game.

We went ahead early, but late in the game, Perkins ran a kickoff back for a touchdown. He went a hundred yards from his own end zone to ours, and I don't think any of our players touched him. There was only a minute and a half to go in the ball game when they kicked off to us. We ran it back to the right side of the field, and from there Jimmy Walden, who was our quarterback then and later coached for me at Nebraska, took off on the first play, a bootleg to the right. They called Walden the "Mississippi Gambler" because he was from Mississippi and he took many chances as a quarterback — he passed for about 900 yards in 1959. Dickie Hamilton, the right halfback, came around to the left on a transcontinental. He got by Perkins, who was still puffing from running the kickoff back, and went for the touchdown. We won the game, 25-20, and had another conference championship. We won four in the five years we were at Wyoming.

One unique thing I remember about that 1959 team was that Jimmy Walden set a school record for attempting two-point conversions. I went back and looked it up once; Jimmy went for the two points 13 times that season and converted seven of them. That's a pretty good percentage. If we had kicked all 13 successfully, we would still have been one point short of what we got going for two.

Looking back, I think Hamilton, the kid who scored that winning touchdown against New Mexico, was the best money player we ever had at Wyoming; in fact, he was one of the best I ever saw. He was a tough little guy who was a good pool player, too. I remember one night, actually it must have been about three in the morning, Carl Selmer and I and a couple of other guys were down in an all-night pool hall in Laramie where Hamilton was playing pool. We wagered on him, and I don't think he let us down. He was a good one. I don't know what ever became of him.

Probably the best football players we had at Wyoming while I was the head coach were Jerry Hill, a halfback who had played six-man football in high school at Lingle, Wyoming; Mark Smolinski, a fullback who was from Rogers City, Michigan; and Chuck Lamson, who transferred from Iowa State as a quarterback. His dad was an assistant basketball coach at Iowa State at the time. Those three players were as good as we had out there, and they all went on to play professional football.

Lamson played on our 1961 team, which beat Air Force and North Carolina State again and tied a good Kansas team, 6-6, in Lawrence. John Hadl was the quarterback at Kansas then, and Curtis McClinton was a running back. They finished the season 7-3-1, including a big win over Nebraska, and beat Rice in the Bluebonnet Bowl.

That last Wyoming team of mine won six games, lost one, and tied two.

In 1960, we were 8-2. We had another tragic situation that year after the Texas Tech game. Tech had a good team; E.J. Holub, later a great pro linebacker, played for them, but we beat them 10-7 down in Lubbock. We flew back to Laramie, and a couple of starters — Bill Bolick,

who had just gotten out of the service and was playing
guard for us, and Sandy Meggert, a halfback — took off for
Colorado. On the way to Denver, they hit a bridge. Bolick
was killed, and Meggert was seriously injured and couldn't
play football after that. Sandy had transferred to Wyoming from Michigan State. His brother played for me when
I was still coaching at Alpena.

We had a pretty good freshman program at Wyoming,
something I tried to emphasize when I came to Nebraska.
We tried to avoid using freshmen on scout squads, figuring
it was better for them not to get discouraged going up
against varsity players every day in practice. We wanted
them to get adjusted, and we wanted them to spend their
first year learning the system. That way they could also
build some confidence. One of the first things we did at Nebraska was change the philosophy regarding freshmen.

While I was at Wyoming I looked into one or two other
college coaching jobs before getting the opportunity to
come to Nebraska. I considered going to the University of
California one time, and I visited the University of Maryland at the end of the 1958 season, while we were getting
ready to play in the Sun Bowl. Tommy Mont had quit at
Maryland, and I think one of his top assistants had been
fired, so I went to College Park to talk with some people
about the Maryland job which Tom Nugent ended up getting. A friend of my uncle was a big shot in the booster club
there, the Terrapin Club, and he told me they had just
hired a new president. Then he said the opening wasn't a
good one anymore, and I gave up on the idea. I was never
really too serious about either of those jobs when it got
right down to it.

While I was at Wyoming, I also went to the University
of Houston to interview for the job that Bill Yeoman got; I
was second again. Bill had been an assistant with me at
Michigan State, and really it was Bill's association with
Michigan State, Biggie Munn and Duffy Daugherty, that
helped Houston finally make it to the big time in college
football. Duffy had Houston on the Michigan State sched-

ule to open the 1967 season, and Houston went up to East
Lansing and beat the Spartans 37-7. What made it even
worse was, Michigan State had been undefeated the previous year — that was the season in which Notre Dame went
for the tie instead of the win at East Lansing. So anyway,
Houston went there and just ran all over Michigan State
with Yeoman's veer offense. The reason it was such an important win was, Houston always had problems getting the
major college football teams to schedule them; they were
indepedent then and didn't join the Southwest Conference
until later.

The Nebraska thing started, when Duffy Daugherty
called Clifford Hardin, who had been the dean of the school
of agriculture at Michigan State before becoming the chancellor at Nebraska. Duffy thought this was a better job
than I did; I was very reluctant about it, in fact, but he
seemed certain this could be a good deal. He told me if I
won here as I had been able to win at Wyoming, things
could go big. There probably wasn't anything Nebraska
wouldn't do for me. I was impressed by the size of the
stadium at Nebraska and the number of people that came
to the games even when things went badly for the team —
at Wyoming, we probably drew an average of 14,000 or
15,000 a game.

Yes, now that I think back on it, Duffy talked me into
pursuing the job at Nebraska.

When I came to Lincoln to talk about the job, I sneaked
into town under an assumed name. I don't remember what
it was, and I don't really know why everyone was so secre-
tive about it. Nebraska talked to John Ralston, a guy I had
coached against at Utah State. I'm not sure if he ever came
for an interview. They also wanted to talk to Ray Nagel;
he was the one they were looking at when they started the
search. Ray was coaching at Utah then. Nebraska might
have talked to Hank Foldberg, who was coaching at Wichita State in 1961, too. I don't know about that, but remember, Tippy Dye, the new athletic director, had come to Nebraska from Wichita State, so he probably did talk to Fold-

My first NU staff: (Back) Melton, Kelly, Corgan, Fischer; (Front) Osborne, Ross, Selmer, Dyer.

berg. Foldberg left Wichita State in 1961. He coached at
Texas A&M in 1962.

We always got total support at Nebraska. When we
came here, there was pressure on the administration to
have a good football program. Nebraska had been a football state for many years, and the fans here hadn't had a
consistent winner since World War II. The team hadn't
been something they could talk about. They had been hir-
ing assistant coaches. Pete Elliott and Bill Jennings had
been assistants, and the administration was looking for
someone who was a head coach.

I remember when I came here to talk about the job at a
dinner at Chancellor Hardin's house, I spilled soup all over
myself. I figured that really got things off to a good start.
But at that time, or right around that time, I talked to
Clarence Swanson, who was head of the regents, and he
told me something that sounded like what Duffy had told
me. Swanson said: "Bob, if you come here and win, you'll
never be sorry. These people want to win that much. You'll
get all the support you need here; you know, whatever you
need we'll try to do." And the regents and administration
always did. Chancellor Hardin was good to me, though I
think he was beginning to wonder a little bit after those
two 6-4 seasons.

Wyoming didn't want to release me from my contract
there, and the whole thing dragged on for a month and a
half. The sportswriters were doing stories every day. The
regents were mad. Everybody in Laramie was mad. They
felt like guys should honor commitments, which I guess I
can understand.

Wyoming has always had people leave. Bowden Wyatt
left. Phil Dickens left. Freddie Akers left. Pat Dye left. But
Wyoming still refuses to believe it's a stepping stone for
coaches. Those people don't even want to think about it.
They got especially mad when I left because they had
presented me a contract that sounded pretty good, one of
those "lifetime" contracts. I hadn't had any interest in
leaving before the Nebraska thing came up, and Wyoming

people were reluctant to let me go to a neighboring state. It looked pretty bad for some time after I left. Wyoming fans were mad at me, and I didn't go back there for a long time. I haven't been back much, except maybe three or four times to speak. By then, people were very nice. I think they had forgotten. As for the job being a stepping stone now, I think if they get a young guy on the way up, it's still going to be one if the guy does a good job. If they get a guy that's going to be running out his string there, it could be more permanent. So far, they've gotten coaches who were intent on moving someplace else.

Jim Ross and I came to Lincoln on the train for our first official press conference at Nebraska. John Melton followed not long after that, and then Carl Selmer. Mike Corgan stayed out in Laramie to see if he or Lloyd Eaton would get the Wyoming job. Mike and Lloyd were the final two candidates, but Mike and Red Jacoby, the athletic director, didn't get along too well at times. Mike could be very outspoken when he wanted to be, and besides that, he used to take some of the compost for his garden from the pile Red kept for sale behind the Wyoming fieldhouse. Red knew Mike was a good coach; that wasn't the problem, but Lloyd had been a very successful head coach at Northern Michigan College, and that gave him an edge in getting the job. So Mike joined Jim, Carl, John and me at Nebraska. Clete Fischer and George Kelly were already here. We kept them from the previous staff. Tom Osborne and Dallas Dyer were our graduate assistants in 1962.

I only had one conversation with Bill Jennings, and that's after I had accepted the job. He was sitting in his office, and I went in to see him. Right away he said: "The first thing you ought to do is get some offices and get rid of this one." He was right. Nebraska had the worst looking football office I had ever seen. It was on the second floor of the Coliseum, down on one end; the place was awful. That was really about all Jennings said to me. We did talk a little bit about some of the players he had. I told him: "With the bunch of kids you have left here, if you'd stay another year, you'd win." He shrugged. I thought Nebraska had good talent, but, you know, when we first looked at the players in spring practice, when we first saw them on the field, we didn't think they were that good. Then, as I got to comparing them with the other Big Eight teams and watching guys like Bill Thornton and Denny Claridge a little more, I started thinking what I told Jennings might have been right.

chapter nine

*Claridge might have been
our greatest quarterback ever;
he just came too soon*

In 11 years at Nebraska, we were cheered for a lot of exciting plays, but we may have been the only team in the history of college football to get a standing ovation for an incomplete pass.

When Dennis Claridge threw the ball on the first play of our first game against South Dakota in 1962, the fans went crazy, even though the pass was incomplete. The year before, Nebraska scored a total of 12 points in five games. The fans didn't think the offense was very imaginative. They were a little itchy to see something other than a handoff. When they did, they let everyone know they approved.

Nebraska won three games the year before I got here. The talent was very good. Bill Jennings was a good football coach and an excellent recruiter. I don't know. Maybe he worked too hard. From what I understand, the coaches and players never took any time to enjoy themselves.

That's one of the most overlooked aspects of a winning program. You have to enjoy what you're doing. You have to be serious and work hard. But you also have to have some fun. Sometimes, having some fun can make you work harder.

At least it worked for me. When I walked down the field and sensed our team lagging, I wasn't afraid to have everyone stop what he was doing. I'd call them together for a few words of wisdom. A player or two were known to catch hell. I wasn't afraid to pinpoint one guy and make him feel responsible for the way things were going. But they weren't always chewing out sessions. A lot of times, I'd just tell the team a funny story. It would loosen them up. They'd start back into practice with a little more determination. It was a simple piece of strategy. But it worked.

It was particularly effective with those first few teams we had at Nebraska. When we first came in, we couldn't believe how poor the facilities were. They were miserable, compared to what we had at Wyoming. We were impressed with the size and the speed of the players, though.

I remember someone coming up to the coaches and asking us why we thought it was a good move going from Wyoming to Nebraska. Jim Ross had the best answer. He said if we didn't win here, it was the dumbest thing we'd ever do in our lives.

If we were going to win, we knew we had to take a totally different philosophy. We talked to the players and they told us that Jennings practiced them three hours straight, sometimes longer. They scrimmaged a lot. They said by the time they were ready to play a game, they were tired, beat up and pretty much emotionally drained.

I guess the previous coaching staff used to square off with some of the players like they were going to fight. There was a lot of bickering. I think that was the biggest thing. By the time we arrived, they were glad to see anybody.

You need good, well-paid coaches. They have to be loyal to the cause. But, more than anything, you need good

This is Dennis Claridge, operator. I don't want long distance.
I want the coaches in the press box.

morale. You can have the best players in the world and lose if they won't play for you. It's like the dogfood salesman. His boss says, "We've got the best dogfood on the market, right?" The salesman says, "Right." The boss says, "And we've got the best salesmen, right?" And the salesman says, "Right." Then the boss says, "Well, how come we don't sell more dogfood?" And the salesman says, "Well, I guess it's because the damn dogs won't eat it." If you're going to win, the good players have to play for you.

Like new coaching staffs at most places, we had a new wave of enthusiasm. The kids wanted to know when we were going to practice and what they could do to get ready. We told them practices would be only an hour and a half to two hours and there wouldn't be any contact once the season started. Everyone would be treated fairly and equally.

The older players worked hard. They were willing to start from scratch. We ended up playing a couple older guys who probably never would have played in the old regime — guys like Jed Rood at guard and Al Fischer at tackle.

Even though we cut the practices almost in half, I still think we worked 'em too hard that first year. We worked the hell out of them. When we first saw the players, we were disappointed. We thought they were going to be a crappy football team. But the more we were around them, the more we realized that this was a pretty good bunch of football players.

Dennis Claridge was the first quarterback I had at Nebraska. I know the fans have read and heard a lot about Jerry Tagge and Van Brownson. But Claridge had just as much going for him. If we'd done the things then that we did later on, there's no doubt in my mind that he might have been the best quarterback we ever had.

He was a winner. I still remember him running down the sideline against Colorado and the ball shoots straight up in the air. Claridge reached back, caught it and didn't even break stride on his way to the end zone.

I also remember how poorly I felt when Claridge played

for me in the East-West All-American Game in Buffalo. I was head coach for the West. John Bridgers of Baylor and John McKay of USC were my assistants. Bridgers coached Don Trull, the All-American quarterback from Baylor. I thought Claridge was better, but I decided to play Trull the first half and Claridge the second half. We lost the first half and Claridge took us right down the field and got us right back in the game in the second half. He did a helluva job. We got down close to the goal line and I let Bridgers talk me into putting Trull in for Claridge because Trull was a dropback passer and Denny wasn't. Well, the first damn thing Trull does is throw an interception. Jay Wilkinson, Bud's son, intercepted the ball on an out pattern in the end zone. Jay played for Duke. It never should have happened. We had those two backs from Arizona State, Tony Lorick and Charley Taylor. We should have rushed all over 'em and kept Claridge in there. I felt terrible. I apologized to Denny after the game.

I still apologize to him when I see him, but I think it hurt me more than it hurt him. He thinks I let him punt in the game just because he was from Nebraska. Dave Parks of Texas Tech punted a lot better than him in practice. McKay was in charge of our kicking game. Claridge kept kicking the ball off the side of his foot. He looked just terrible in practice. McKay told me we had to get another kicker and I told him to wait and see how he punts in the game. Claridge didn't let me down. He averaged about 50 yards a punt in that ball game. He kicked the heck out of the ball. He was just a great athlete.

Although I didn't recruit Claridge, he was one of several good, big football players from Minnesota. We always liked to recruit up there and still do, especially those big farm kids. It was easy. We'd drive along the country roads and look for young guys plowing the fields. We'd stop and ask directions to the nearest big city, like Minneapolis. If the kid put down the plow and pointed his finger in the direction of the city, we'd thank him and drive on. But if he picked up the plow and used it to point, we'd try to sign him to a letter of intent right on the spot.

Once we recruited a player, it was easy to tell the backs from the linemen. We'd just run 'em into the woods. The ones who ran around the trees were the backs. The ones who ran over the trees and knocked 'em down were the linemen.

I inherited a great athlete that first year at fullback. He could knock down trees . . . and run around 'em. I'd heard all about Bill "Thunder" Thornton outrushing the Heisman Trophy winner, Ernie Davis, when Nebraska played Syracuse in 1961.

I guess his high school coach in Toledo, Ohio, nicknamed him Thunder when he was just a freshman because he was so explosive. I don't know how he got such a clever nickname. I remember a player from the same section of Ohio who played for us at Michigan State. We called him John "Thunder" Lewis. I've always wondered if we didn't come up with that nickname first.

I think it fit Thunder Thornton better, though. Even though he didn't play much for me that first year, I could tell he was a helluva football player. I could see why he led the team in rushing as a sophomore and a junior. He dislocated his shoulder before the season started. But he still played against Michigan in the second game.

That was an unforgettable game at Ann Arbor. I'm not so sure I don't cherish it as much as any game I ever coached. The win over LSU in the Orange Bowl was important because it gave us our first national championship. The win over Oklahoma in 1971 was important because that's the game everyone still talks about. But the win over Michigan is the one that put us on the map. It showed the country that we were turning things around. I think the players knew how much the game meant to me. They saw how much attention was devoted to it. The Detroit writers were calling it a homecoming for Bob Devaney. It was Band Day and they had a big crowd. It was a great atmosphere to pull one off for a team not used to winning.

We felt we had to set some kind of a goal. The coaches —

Dennis Claridge sets off on his 68-yard touchdown run in the 1964 Orange Bowl to beat Auburn.

Mike Corgan, George Kelly, Jim Ross, Clete Fischer, John Melton, Carl Selmer and Tom Osborne — didn't think we were quite good enough to win the Big Eight or go undefeated. So we never talked like that. We just talked about how we were going down to Michigan in front of all those people and beat 'em in their own backyard. We watched a lot of film on Michigan and we didn't think they were that great.

A lot of our players were from that general area. Thornton's mother was at the game. So were a lot of other players' parents. I remember leading Michigan, 7-6, at the half and sensing the upset. I don't remember exactly what I said at halftime. But I remember reminding everyone how much a win would mean for our program.

We won, 25-13. Dennis Stuewe had a touchdown and rushed for about 80 yards. But everyone was talking about Thunder Thornton. He scored a couple touchdowns — one was 16 yards — and his blocking was just ferocious, despite an injured shoulder.

Bill was one of our first captains. He was a real smart guy — the first black elected into the Innocents Society at Nebraska. He was a real leader, but he had to play hurt. He got hurt again when we lost to Missouri and missed the next two games. Because he was hurt, we just didn't get the great things out of Bill that he had done before we got here. I never lost my respect for him, though. I wasn't a bit surprised to see him last six years with the St. Louis Cardinals. He could run and he'd hit you.

When Thornton was hurt, we used Rudy Johnson some at fullback. Kent McCloughan alternated at both halfbacks, besides playing a lot on defense. Dennis Stuewe didn't get that much ink, but he was a much underrated halfback. I'll never forget that first year when he bailed us out against North Carolina State. They had a little scatback named Joe Scarpati. He returned a kickoff 91 yards for a touchdown against us in the third quarter. It put us in a hole, 14-7. Stuewe had to score twice in the last quarter for us to win, 19-14. We were behind 14-13 and needed Claridge

Come on! A little mud never hurt anybody.

to engineer a sensational drive at the end. We were third and long and North Carolina State was looking for a pass. But Stuewe scored on a sweep play with a minute left. While everyone relaxed, North Carolina State ran back another kickoff. When the game ended, they were inside our five. I'm glad we had Stuewe. He was a fine competitor.

McCloughan could run, too. But I never realized he was going to be as great as he turned out to be. We weren't hurting for backs. Rudy Johnson was a fine right halfback or fullback. He could do a lot of things. Willie Ross was the left halfback. Warren Powers and Dave Theisen were behind him. We had some pretty good ends, too. Jim Huge was one. Bill Comstock and Larry Donovan, both from Scottsbluff, Larry Tomlinson and Dick Callahan were others. In the line, we had Bob Brown. Lloyd Voss, Tyrone Robertson, Larry Kramer and John Kirby. Kramer was an All-American in the offensive line, but he played like an All-American on defense, too. Thinking back, we had some outstanding linemen . . . Dwain Carlson . . . Ron Michka . . . Lyle Sittler. Michka was first string center. Sittler and Jim Baffico were behind him.

Baffico was a real character. He transferred from some junior college in San Francisco. He could play the piano and I guess you could say he was a literary sort of person because he was writing and acting in all the university plays. The fans liked him because he weighed 265 pounds and he was only 6-1. He was our kicker by default. I'll never forget his first punt in the first offensive series of the Oklahoma game. We went into the game thinking we might win. It would have tied us for the championship. But Oklahoma blocked the punt, went in and scored and we were never in the ball game.

That was the third kicking job Baffico lost. Early in the season, we had to replace him with John Faiman as the extra point kicker. He was our kickoff man until he kicked the ball out-of-bounds four times in a row at Colorado. I have to laugh. Baffico had a harder time kicking than he did staying eligible. If he wasn't at Casey's drinking a beer, he was at an all-night truck stop eating breakfast. He had a lot of talent. He just waited to show it. He flunked out of school and became a foot patrolman on the Lincoln Police Force. Then he went and played three years for the Buffalo Bills. They had a couple of AFL championship teams while he was there. Nobody heard much about him again until a year or two ago. It turns out that he came back to Nebraska, got a master's degree, then went to Michigan and got his doctorate. He taught drama a few years at Georgia, then moved to Pittsburgh. He's a very successful man today. He directs 'Another World' on television and he's directed a few movies. One was 'The Fish That Saved Pittsburgh.'

That first year was very successful and a lot of fun. We might have created some false illusions by going 6-0. We didn't get beat until November. Missouri beat us in our homecoming game, 16-7. Nebraska hadn't scored on Missouri in four years ... until Noel Martin intercepted a pass and returned it 88 yards in the second quarter. Noel is Bill Jennings' son-in-law. I guess he was just trying to help me along. We were tied, 7-7, at halftime. But that was the game where the officials gave Johnny Roland a 46-yard touchdown even though he fumbled the ball into the end zone.

Roland, though, was probably the best back we had to face that first year, but there were some other good ones — Dave Hoppmann, the Iowa State quarterback; Jim Grisham and Joe Don Looney of Oklahoma; and, of course, Gale Sayers of Kansas. The Big Eight wasn't a bad league. It wasn't easy to sneak up on anybody. Our players had to work awfully hard.

chapter ten

*I invented a pro scout
to motivate Bob Brown;
he was always injured*

Bob Brown is one of the most famous players I've ever coached, but he was also a problem at first. He had all the God-given talent in the world. He was the best two-way player I ever coached. He built his reputation as a great offensive lineman, but he was a great linebacker, too. I enjoyed watching him become a consistent all-pro, especially after all the growing pains he went through at Nebraska. I'm only being honest when I say that Bob Brown was a head case when we first got here. We had a hard time getting him to practice. He was either hurt or didn't want to play. If you wanted to find him, you looked in the training room first.

I didn't know what to do with him. One day, he was in the training room, getting taped, and said he didn't think he could practice. I told him he didn't have to practice, but to put on his uniform and come out anyway and watch. I got out there before he did and saw some guy standing over

Bob Brown, disguising himself as a towel rack? Well, he was a character and a darn good football player, too.

on the sidelines in a three-piece suit and got an idea. I went over to Brown and said: "You see that guy over there?" And Brown said: "Yeah." I said: "He's a scout from the Philadelphia Eagles. He's been asking about you. He's been concerned about you."

Hell, I didn't know the guy from Adam. I told Bob that this guy was interested in him but concerned about his being injury-prone and not practicing very often and that the pros probably would stay clear of him. Then I walked away. Bob came over to me and said: "Just a minute, coach. Maybe I can go today."

It was amazing. Brown went out that day and just beat the hell out of everybody who came near him. I couldn't believe it. He'd tear somebody apart, then look over and see if this guy was watching him. After that, I actually did talk to some pro scouts. I asked them to talk to Brown about his great talent and his need to overcome the injury factor.

Up until that time, most of the coaches had just about given up on Bob Brown. Clete Fischer even told us once to forget about him because he was useless. The modern coaching term for him would be looks like Tarzan, but plays like Jane.

I think Bob's brother, Ulysses, drove the coaches crazier than he did. They gave Ulysses a scholarship to get Bob. Ulysses was always hanging around wherever Bob was, even if he was supposed to be somewhere else. Ulysses would leave whatever he was doing and come over and see what was happening to his brother.

Once — God, I'll never forget this — Brown was lying down there on the ground with the wind knocked out of him. He kind of looked up and saw his brother standing over him. And he said: "Ulysses, you ought to call Momma. I'm hurt real bad."

I'm not trying to poke fun at Bob Brown. He's a tremendous person and he got his act together before he left us. Some pretty knowledgeable football people still think he's the best offensive lineman ever to play in the NFL. I'd be the last to argue that, but he still did some pretty funny things at Nebraska.

I think my favorite story about Bob Brown was the time we played at Colorado that first year. He came out on the field and said: "This altitude is bad out here; it's real bad." To prove his point, he sprints 100 yards from one end of the football field to the other. And he falls down on the ground and can't get his breath. He thinks it's because of the altitude. But Bob never stopped to realize that he hadn't run that far or that fast any time in his entire life. God, that was funny. I laugh every time I think about that story because I can still see him, gasping for air on the ground. He really thought the altitude did him in.

We honestly didn't know what to do with Brown. He could make a crisis out of a minor bruise. That first spring, I got so mad at him once that I picked up his uniform. He came into my office to find out why. I told him the coaches had decided that he should give up contact sports. I told him that we recommended golf, or maybe tennis, where he could use his strength without getting hurt. He was 6-4 and 270 pounds. He pleaded for us to reinstate him. That fall, he made All-Big Eight. The next year, he was an All-American.

Even though the players knew he was unpredictable, they learned to respect Bob Brown. When he said something, they listened. Before we played Auburn in the '64 Orange Bowl, he told Don Bryant he had asked everyone to play hard for him because he had some deep-seated animosity toward the state of Alabama.

The coaching staff turned Brown around a little, but so did the players. They were so enthusiastic, it had to rub off. The best example of their attitude was the Gotham Bowl. We met with them after Oklahoma beat the hell out of us and tried to discourage them from going to the Gotham Bowl. We told them every bad thing we could think of. We told them it was a "crappy bowl." We told them we didn't know if there was any money. We told them about the newspaper strike in New York. We told them about playing a morning game in a climate just as cold as ours. We even tried to encourage the seniors to vote against the bowl one afternoon at a meeting over at Selleck Quadrangle. I gave them five minutes to talk it over and come up with a decision. They deliberated 15 seconds, then voted unanimously to go.

Bill Thornton said it was the only way for him to get the bad taste of Oklahoma out of his mouth. I remember telling Tyrone Robertson how cold it was going to be and he just rubbed his huge hands together and said the cold wasn't going to slow him down.

This was a good group of people. Stuewe and a bunch of other seniors had been running and lifting weights every day, hoping we'd get a bowl bid. They didn't care about how cold it was going to be. They didn't care about not having any people in the stands or about being the last team in the country invited to a bowl game. They knew Miami had been invited three weeks earlier than they were. The game was December 15th and it was already December 4th. As coaches, we weren't too excited about playing George Mira. We knew he was the best passer in the country. But the players didn't care. The only two things that mattered to them was (1) the game was in New York City and (2) it was going to be on national television.

The whole thing was so shaky, it was scary. We'd heard all about the first game the year before. Utah State and Baylor played in bitterly cold weather at the Polo Grounds. The crowd was below 15,000 and the only thing that kept the promoters from taking a bath in red ink was the national television contract.

Actually, the first Gotham Bowl was supposed to be played the year before that. Oregon State was all set to go and Sonny Grandelius accepted for Colorado. But the Colorado administrators turned their thumbs down and it was too late for the bowl officials to line up another opponent.

The promoters sensed we were leery. They tried to make a big point about moving the game from the Polo Grounds

Waiting in the airport to take off for the Gotham Bowl — if the certified check ever arrives.

to Yankee Stadium. That didn't mean a damn thing to me, especially in the middle of December. But try telling a 21-year-old kid from Nebraska that playing in the same stadium where Babe Ruth played doesn't mean anything. Try telling Nebraska football fans that playing in a bowl game doesn't mean anything. They'd only played in two and never won one. Nebraska fans didn't care how shaky the deal was. Even Frank Morrison, the governor, was yelling for us to go. If we'd have talked the players out of going, we wouldn't have been very popular.

The fans were excited about the Big Eight getting some national prestige. Oklahoma and Alabama were playing in the Orange Bowl and Missouri and Georgia Tech were playing in the Bluebonnet Bowl. When the Gotham Bowl invited us, it was the first time in the history of the league that three teams had bowl bids.

I knew the deck was stacked. I'd heard from a pretty reliable source that the Gotham Bowl was going to guarantee Miami $75,000 and take good care of them. They were going to guarantee us $55,000, but the TV contract went sour. I think ABC finally picked it up for something like $15,000. It was awful. I knew they were headed for another financial bath. New York didn't give a damn about the game. They were moving the kickoff up to 11 o'clock because the New York Titans and the Houston Oilers were playing an AFL playoff game at the Polo Grounds that afternoon. That was our tipoff right there that nobody was going to show . . . that and the newspapers being on strike.

They were ready to accommodate Miami. But I think they were ready to put it to us, if they could get away with it. Finally, I think they said they'd guarantee us $35,000, plus a share of the gate. Hell, there wasn't going to be any gate. And I was curious to see how they were going to come up with $35,000. It was supposed to be a charity game for the March of Dimes and they weren't any more organized than the lady who gets the envelope at work to take around the block.

The university people started to get a little nervous, too.

We sat down with them and the chancellor and talked about it. Finally, we decided we had to have expense money put in escrow before we could leave. Even that got shaky. We didn't know if that game was ever going to come off. Hell, the whole team was out at the airport, waiting to get on the plane and there still wasn't any money in the bank. We must have waited a couple hours. When we heard they had the check, we got on the plane. Then we got another call, saying the check wasn't certified. So we waited some more. We wouldn't let the pilots take off. I still didn't care much about going. But I thought since we'd wasted time practicing and it meant a lot to the kids, we might as well get the show on the road. Finally, someone called and said everything was all set. It had to be the shakiest situation in the history of bowl games.

It was fairly decent for the players. We stayed at the Manhattan Hotel. The team was a special guest one night on "The Johnny Carson Show." They got to see the Statue of Liberty, the Empire State Building, Madison Square Garden and the Stork Club. I think some of them went to the Peppermint Lounge so they could do the twist. God, that seems like a long time ago. The twist and crewcuts. Life was a little simpler back then. A dangerous drug in those days was a sleeping pill.

Anyway, back to the game. The weather was terrible, just like we thought it would be. They said they had 6,000 paid admissions and 5,000 kids they let in free. That would have made about 11,000 people in a 63,000-seat stadium. If that was true, about 10,000 of them went home before kick-off. There wasn't even next of kin out there.

It was a miserable, cold, dreary morning. I do remember my pre-game pep talk, though. I told the players that the weather was terrible and the game didn't seem like a very big deal because nobody was out there. Then I said it reminded me of the days when I was a kid and we used to have fights in the back alley. There wouldn't be anyone watching there either, but pride was still the most important thing in the world. In 1962, you could give that kind of a talk and it would fire your players up. Ten years later, when we won the national championship, it might not have worked because kids had become more sophisticated.

We needed some fire that day. It was snowing and we were freezing. If New York can have a bowl game, so can Nebraska. Or Antarctica. We had heaters by the bench and we had a helluva time getting the substitutes into the ball game. They didn't want to leave the heaters.

We knew Mira would be great, but he was even a little better than great that day. We tried everything but the Peace Corps to stop him. We blitzed. We crashed our ends. We yielded short to protect long. But he kept throwing those line drives and completing them. I'd hate to have been one of his receivers. Mira could sting your hands on a nice day. On a cold day like that, those guys' hands probably got so numb they didn't know they had any.

Mira threw 46 times and completed 24 for 321 yards and a couple touchdowns. As far as I was concerned, we were lucky to get away with that. Old George had at least five passes dropped because it was so damn cold. Once, one of his receivers fell down at the goal line waiting for a cinch touchdown pass. We didn't have anybody within 20 yards of him.

That was one of the craziest games you'll ever see. Both teams pulled everything in the book. Miami faked a field goal and ran two Statue of Liberty plays. We faked a punt and ran a Statue of Liberty play. The game went back and forth like a teeter-totter. It was 6-6 at the quarter, 20-20 at the half and 28-27 after three quarters. It's hard to believe they outgained us 502 to 296 and we won, 36-34. Willie Ross had a 92-yard kickoff return and we made a couple two-point conversions in the second half. They were the difference.

Mira was brilliant. Red Smith was one of the sportswriters at the game and he said it was the greatest college quarterback performance in New York since Johnny Lujack played for Notre Dame in 1946. He said the game was better than some of the greatest games the New York

The Gotham Bowl in Yankee Stadium. Frigid and freezing. And more snow than fans. Count 'em.

Giants had played in Yankee Stadium.

Fortunately, we intercepted a couple of Mira's passes. Claridge intercepted one and guess who intercepted the other pass in the last minute of the game? Bob Brown himself. It didn't stop me, though, from doing something I rarely did as a coach. I went over to George Mira after the game and congratulated him. I'm not so sure that wasn't the greatest individual performance we ever had to put up with.

Naturally, the win made everyone forget about all the financial problems of the Gotham Bowl and everything else. We were luckier than hell, but we won it. People acted like we had just won the Orange Bowl or the World Series. I didn't realize it at the time, but that game was really important for our program. It gave Nebraska its best record since 1905. But more important, it helped generate the enthusiasm that carried over the next few years.

One thing people forget is that we did use the Gotham Bowl to recruit. We'd already recruited some great players — people like Tony Jeter, Freeman White, Harry Wilson. They were a good base to help us recruit some more.

The Gotham Bowl died a natural death because it was such a financial disaster. I remember Bob Curran, the executive director, when they handed out the watches at the awards banquet. Hell, he'd had it. He was swimming in debt. All our players didn't even get watches. I don't think Claridge even got one. If he did, someone else gave it to him.

The Gotham Bowl had promised to pay for a bunch of meals, but they couldn't come through. We were on our own a few times. We all went out and celebrated the night we won. The coaches took their wives to some expensive club. When the bill came for everyone to split up, Clete Fischer owed about 50 bucks ... and all he'd had was a 7-Up.

Willie Ross was the best story, though. Before the game, Clarence Swanson, a Nebraska regent and owner of Hovland-Swanson clothing store, walked in the locker room wearing a real nice cashmere sweater. Willie noticed it and mentioned how much he liked it. Swanson told Willie that if he had a good day in the Gotham Bowl, maybe he could get him one. Well, Willie ran a kickoff back for a touchdown and led us in rushing with 77 yards. He did everything. He was probably our biggest hero. That next Monday after we got back, Swanson left word for Willie to pick out a sweater. So Willie goes down and picks out the most expensive sweater in the store. I mean it was like $200. Willie recognized quality.

They called Willie "The Twister." He was an exciting runner who finally learned to quit dancing and turn upfield. I really got a kick out of Willie Ross. I'll never forget that first Orange Bowl game when they took the players to several gambling things. They went to the horse races, the dog races and jai alai. These kids were all broke, especially Willie. He lost everything, even the expense money we gave him. He was borrowing money the third day he was there. One day, he went out deep-sea fishing. He caught a big sailfish and was just beaming. When he took it back to the dock, he asked the guy how much it would cost to mount it and the guy says "about $136." Willie looks at him for a couple seconds, then says: "Cut her loose!" He was just broke as hell.

chapter eleven

*He had to be the
smallest all-conference fullback
in major college history*

Frank Solich was quite a football player for his size. In fact, he was quite a football player, period. We recruited him out of Holy Name High School in Cleveland, Ohio, where he was all-league and all-state, and, I think probably, a high school All-American. Frank scored over 100 points when he was a senior and led his team to the city championship, but it was actually another player at Holy Name, named Mike Worley, that we were interested in when we saw Frank. Worley was a tough, hard-nosed kid himself, but whenever we'd watch films of Holy Name's games, we'd keep noticing Solich, who was a tailback. He was small, but in those days, we could take about as many players as we wanted. The NCAA scholarship limit was 45, so we thought we might as well take a chance on this little guy who really wanted to play college football but who was ignored by all the other major colleges. Here was a kid who didn't get another major college offer, yet he came to Ne-

Frank Solich, not a good "little" football player, just plain good.

braska and became an All-Big Eight fullback. He was a tremendous inspiration to the other players. Frank never said much, but he was tough. I can remember his being injured only twice. When he was a sophomore, he broke his ankle in the second game of the year, against Minnesota, and then in the Orange Bowl game, after the 1965 season, he hurt his knee. Other than that, I don't think Frank was ever out of a game because of an injury.

Incidentally, we should have won that Orange Bowl, but we lost to Alabama, 39-28, because I was outcoached and our team was outplayed. Alabama played a super game, and Steve Sloan, their quarterback, threw the football better than he had ever thrown it in his life. I was outcoached in that we hadn't prepared our players for onside kicks. Alabama noticed that one of our up-front players always turned his back when he dropped back to block on kickoff returns, and they kicked toward him. They recovered three onside kicks in that game, and they used a tackle-eligible pass play that we didn't defense at all well.

Anyway, getting back to Solich, the most serious of his two injuries was the broken ankle because that kept him out for several games in 1963. We tried to get a hardship ruling for him that year, to get him an extra season of eligibility, but since he was playing in the second game when he got hurt, they wouldn't grant him a hardship. According to the rule, he would have had to get hurt in the first game. Frank came back late in the season, and we thought he might be a little gun-shy, but he wasn't. In that Orange Bowl game against Auburn, he ran a punt back about 80 yards for a touchdown, but the official ruled he had stepped out-of-bounds and brought it back.

To digress from Solich again for a minute and talk about our efforts at having perfect seasons the next two years, after that Orange Bowl, as I've said, we had several players go into pro ball and the next year we had a lot of holes to fill. Even though we had some close games, we won our first nine in 1964 and had wrapped up at least a share of the Big Eight championship before we went to Oklahoma for our final regular-season game. That's the one in which Oklahoma put in a couple of sophomores to replace Lance Rentzel and Jim Grisham — the guy who replaced Grisham was named Jon Kennedy, a fullback — and wound up beating us when they shouldn't have. The score was 17-7. Fortunately for us, Missouri beat Kansas, 34-14, that day or Kansas would have tied us for the conference championship. Anyway, then we went to the Cotton Bowl for the first time and played a good game even though we lost to Arkansas, 10-7, in the last five minutes when a guy named Bobby Burnett scored a touchdown. We held Arkansas to less than 50 yards rushing, but they were a little better at passing than we were that day.

That reminds me of a story I used to tell about myself after one of our games out in Wyoming. I was getting off the train after a game in which we had not gained very many yards and lost, and I bumped into this little old lady.

I said: "Excuse me, mam."

"Where do you think you're going, young man?" she asked.

"Nowhere," I said.

"Oh, you must be another one of those Wyoming running backs," she replied.

Anyway, I've always considered the significant thing about that 1964 season to be our quarterback situation. Fred Duda, who had been the backup for Denny Claridge the year before, was our starter. He was from Chicago. About three games into the schedule, we went over to Iowa State and Duda broke his leg. I had to send in Bobby Churchich, who hadn't played a single down other than in the opening game against South Dakota. Well, the first couple of plays Bobby called he seemed to be looking to the other players in the huddle, saying: "Is that play okay with you guys?" Pretty soon, Larry Kramer, one of the big linemen, said to Bob: "Look, don't worry about what these clowns think. You call the damn plays, you're the quarterback, and we'll run 'em." From that point on, Churchich took charge. He not only did a good job of beating Iowa State, 14-7, but he took us to the conference title and almost directed us to an unbeaten season. Bobby was a real good quarterback — he came from Omaha North High School — but at that time, he was only a sophomore and he was untried. Bobby Churchich really came through for us in 1964.

That was a key year for us because there we were rebuilding after losing all those seniors the year before, yet we wound up with a 9-2 record. I knew right then Nebraska could stay very representative from that year on. The 1964 team also gave us a good nucleus to build around for 1965. The '65 team should have been national champions. We were 10-0 until we lost in the Orange Bowl to Alabama, and we had one heck of a team. We'd have been national champions, of course, if we had won that game. The top two teams in the ratings ahead of us, Michigan State and Arkansas, both got beat before we played our game. UCLA beat Michigan State in the Rose Bowl, and Arkansas lost to LSU in the Cotton Bowl, so the stage was set for us. In 1965, Churchich and Duda alternated at quarterback, which was both a good and bad situation. When we came to the Orange Bowl, Churchich probably should have started, but Duda was a senior and, not that I'm superstitious or anything like that, but you know Fred Duda had never lost a game in which he had started — high school or college — until that night in Miami. It was one of those things that backfired. Well, things started off bad and got worse in that game. We finally got Churchich in there, and he set an Orange Bowl record for touchdown passes with three of them, two to Tony Jeter. He came in to complete 12 of 17 passes for 232 yards, most of them coming in the second half. But we had fallen behind 24-7 by halftime and we couldn't come back.

We were 10-0 going into the 1966 Orange Bowl, and UCLA and Louisiana State had given us a chance to win the national championship by winning their bowl games against the teams ahead of us in the ratings. Those were

Dennis Claridge carries the Orange Bowl trophy (January 1964) off the plane after our return to Lincoln.

the same ingredients that finally led to our first national championship following the 1970 season, when we beat LSU 17-12 in the Orange Bowl. Earlier that day Texas lost to Notre Dame in the Cotton Bowl and Ohio State lost to Stanford in the Rose Bowl. The difference was, that this time we took advantage of it.

To get back to Frank Solich, he was on those two teams that nearly made it through the entire year without losing and almost was part of a national championship team. In Frank's three varsity seasons, we were 29-4. The only game we lost when he was a sophomore was to Air Force, 17-13, here in Lincoln. His senior year against the Air Force, out in Colorado Springs, Frank gained 204 yards, which was a modern Nebraska single-game record that stood up until 1976 when Richard Berns gained 211 yards against Hawaii. Frank's record held up for 11 years.

Frank was real quick, but you might wonder why we'd play a little guy like that at fullback. He was about 5-7 or 5-8 and he weighed about 150 pounds. At that time, we had a spread formation, of which Tom Osborne still runs a variation. The fullback lined up right behind the quarterback. We ran a lot of option plays to the fullback, and we'd release a guy downfield to keep the defensive backs from coming up. Also, in our T-formation, the halfbacks carried a lot of the blocking load. We had to make some blocking adjustments, but when Frank had to, he could block pretty well. He was a good all-around football player. He could catch the ball, and he was fast — we had recruited him primarily as a specialty man, to return punts and kickoffs and to be a spot player. I remember in the Minnesota game in 1964, up in Minneapolis, they were able to handle most of what we tried against them, but when we put Frank in at fullback for the first time and flanked both of our ends, with halfbacks in the slots in that spread formation, it drove Minnesota crazy. If Minnesota brought their linebackers up close to the line of scrimmage, we'd just send Frank through on some quick-openers. His first move was very explosive. Well, with about seven or eight minutes left to play, we were behind by nine points. Fred Duda was the quarterback, and he was supposed to pass, but the play broke down and Solich was his only possible receiver. Duda hit him on a 45-yard touchdown pass, and we came back to win the game, 26-21. Frank could do a lot of things. The next year, in 1965, he was chosen the All-Big Eight fullback. He had to be the smallest all-conference fullback in major college history.

I've told this story many times, but Frank was determined not to be the smallest player in the league. We had a defensive back named Larry Wachholtz, who was from North Platte, and Larry wasn't very big either. Frank figured he could be a little heavier than Larry by taping some weights inside his shorts when it came time to weigh in at the beginning of the season. He had to be pretty careful when he got on the scales, but Frank gave it a try and I forget exactly how much he weighed. Maybe it was 155 pounds or something like that. Well, then Wachholtz got on the scales and he weighed about a pound more, so Solich was still the smallest guy on the team.

Speaking of that, it reminds me of another story. Don Faurot was the athletic director at Missouri about that time, and he raised a big ruckus about false weights appearing in game programs. He claimed everybody wasn't weighing their players accurately, so the Big Eight instituted what they called a "true weight." You were supposed to weigh your players in front of the news media. So we had all the local sportswriters come over to the stadium, and we weighed everybody in front of them ... and up stepped Solich with a couple of five-pound weights taped under his gray shorts. He didn't want to be the littlest guy in the league.

Frank wasn't big enough to play pro football, but he's been a very successful coach both in high school and now at Nebraska. To give you some idea of what kind of a class guy he is, let me tell you another story I once heard about Frank. He was coaching in high school and had a real good team. His team had just beaten another team that had a good back, who had played pretty well in a losing effort. So after the game, one of Frank's players was talking to a newspaper fellow, and he was telling this newspaper guy that the other team's running back hadn't been so good. He said they'd handled him all right. Well, Frank heard this and he came right over to that kid, grabbed him and said: "You never downgrade an opponent like that. You always respect your opponents." Then the kid told the writer, "Actually, that running back was pretty good." Frank always wants his players to conduct themselves in a proper manner. We were real happy to get him to come back to Nebraska and coach for us.

chapter twelve

*Anybody who knows
Monte Kiffin can
believe that*

Despite what you may have heard, it isn't just the head coach who makes a good football team. You've got to have good assistant coaches, who are loyal to you. That's one area in which I was always very fortunate. In addition to Tom Osborne, three of my other assistants went on to become head football coaches in Division I of the NCAA: Warren Powers, Monte Kiffin, and Jim Walden. All of them, except Tom, played for me, too, and I'll tell you what, when you talk about fine athletes, you've got to include Jimmy Walden. He was an excellent quarterback for us at Wyoming, a real good one.

Jimmy was a very fine passer, and he could run. He played in Canada for three or four years before he started coaching in high school in Mississippi, where he grew up. Walden took an assistant's job at the University of Miami not long after we beat Notre Dame in the Orange Bowl. Carl Selmer already had announced he was going there, and Jimmy joined him. Monte Kiffin was at Louisville interviewing for a job open there at the time; Lee Corso had just left for Indiana. Walden had been an assistant to Warren Powers for a year at Washington State when Warren left for Missouri, and they gave the head coach's job to him. Washington State said they picked Walden because they were sold on the Nebraska system Warren had brought in there the year before. They said it was a great system, and Jimmy hadn't gotten his nickname as a Mississippi gambler for nothing.

Monte Kiffin wanted a head coaching job bad. I think when he was recruited by Bill Jennings to come to Nebraska, he wanted to be a football coach someday, and he tried hard to get several jobs that came open. In addition to the Louisville job, Monte's name was mentioned, at one time or another, for jobs at Virginia Tech, Memphis State, Oregon, and Michigan State while he was here, and then after he went to Arkansas as an assistant to Lou Holtz, I know he interviewed for jobs at Colorado, Kansas State, and Minnesota before he got the one at North Carolina State. Michigan State asked permission to talk to Monte when Denny Stolz left and they hired Darryl Rogers. Monte finally left Nebraska because he figured maybe if he went to another school, he'd have experience at two different places and that would help him get a head coach's job. We tried hard for Monte, and he's a fine football coach. I'm sure he'll be successful at North Carolina State.

Monte played on our 1963 team that had all those great seniors. That was in the days of the war between the American Football League and the National Football League, and we were surrounded by pro scouts all fall. They were everywhere. There were just droves of them at the Orange Bowl, and when that game ended, the scouts all hit our locker room and were in there trying to sign our guys before they could even shower. It was almost a locker room riot, with people from both pro leagues and the Canadian league in there trying to get the same players. Bob Brown was a hot prospect, and he was drafted No. 1 by both the

Monte Kiffin: Oklahoma wound up on probation after trying to recruit him.

Philadelphia Eagles and the Denver Broncos. He signed with the Eagles later that night in the lobby of our hotel and became an all-pro player. I think finally we had 11 of our 13 senior players sign or try to play pro football; six of them signed that night. Auburn had a couple of players signed, too. From our team, Lloyd Voss signed with the Green Bay Packers; Bob Jones signed with the Washington Redskins; Willie Ross signed with the Buffalo Bills; and John Kirby signed with the Minnesota Vikings. Later, Denny Claridge and Rudy Johnson also signed, and Larry Tomlinson and Dave Theisen both played in Canada. Monte Kiffin was a second-string tackle at Nebraska, but he was signed to a pro contract that night by the Minnesota Vikings. He never played for them, though. He was a graduate assistant for us in 1964 and then played for Winnipeg in the Canadian League before coming back here as an assistant freshman coach. He was also the freshman baseball coach here one year.

Of course, everyone knows the most famous story about Monte, and I hope he won't get upset with my telling it again; he's a lot different person now, but before the Gotham Bowl game after the 1962 season, Monte got a little carried away one night. It was the night of the senior party; they used to hold it down at the University Club in those days. A bunch of players left the party and went to a little all-night cafe located near a dairy. After they got something to eat, they decided they didn't want to walk all the way back to campus, so Monte went across the street to the dairy and "borrowed" a milk truck. The truck was full of players when the police pulled it over, but most of the other players were running backs who were fast enough that they took off running and got away. No policeman was going to catch the other kids, but Monte was stuck. He was too slow to get away. Of course, I had to hand out some punishment for his indiscretion, so we didn't take him to New York City for the Gotham Bowl. I'll tell you, though, that made a man out of Monte Kiffin, and the next year he played just super for us.

I heard when he got to North Carolina State, he did things like taking his team to the beach to swim one day when it was too hot to practice; he even drove one of the team buses to get to the seashore. He rode a fire engine to a pep rally another time. Monte has changed, but he's still a character. I read where one day he put on a mask like the Lone Ranger and rode around campus at North Carolina State on a white horse. The band was playing by the student union and up rode the new football coach, trying to publicize his team's spring game. Monte set up a draft for that spring game; they drafted everybody, trainers, student managers, sports information directors, administrators ... The winners ate steaks served by the losers, who ate hotdogs. The final score was 37-34. It all sounds like something Monte would do. He also was supposed to have jumped out of an airplane and boxed with Joe Frazier. I guess some of the players called his practices "Monte's Marathons" they were so long. Monte can be a pretty strict coach, but his first team was supposed to finish last in the conference and it won six games, so he must have known what he was doing. When Guy Ingles left to join him as an assistant coach, he said Monte's enthusiasm was contagious. Monte was talking about going to bowl games and winning national championships right away. Anybody who knows Monte Kiffin can believe that.

The recruiting of Monte is another interesting story, especially considering the football rivalry between Nebraska and Oklahoma. Bill Jennings, the head coach at Nebraska then, had been on Bud Wilkinson's staff at Oklahoma. They were both recruiting Monte, who was an all-state athlete at Lexington, and they had a real recruiting war. The result of it all was, Oklahoma was put on probation because of Monte. Jennings was pretty upset over the whole deal with Kiffin because he said Wilkinson had promised not to come into Nebraska to try to get Monte. Jennings claimed it was Wilkinson's policy not to try to recruit a player from Nebraska, who was interested in going there, unless he had first informed the University he intended to do so. If that's true, things have really changed in recruiting. As I heard the story, Jennings wrote Wilkinson a letter telling him he had gone back on his word about recruiting Kiffin and if Wilkinson wasn't going to keep his word, he was going to report Oklahoma to the NCAA for some recruiting violations while he was on the staff. Jennings had been in charge of recruiting at Oklahoma, and there was supposed to have been some fund they used for transportation for prospective athletes. The NCAA rule was later changed and became more in line with what Oklahoma had done. Anyway, Jennings supposedly sent a letter to Wilkinson. Bud, being a very astute fellow, sent a copy of Jennings' letter to the NCAA along with a letter of his own, saying something like Coach Jennings apparently knows about some infractions the University of Oklahoma is supposed to have committed when he was on our staff, that I know nothing about, and we would certainly like for you to get to the bottom of this. That put Jennings in a corner, but he always maintained that he had not turned Oklahoma in.

Jennings really must have enjoyed the time his Nebraska team beat Wilkinson and Oklahoma here in Lincoln to end the Sooners' long conference winning streak. That happened in 1959.

Warren Powers might have been a freshman or a redshirt on that 1959 team because he was already here when we came from Wyoming. They tell me he was a 155-pound quarterback in high school, in Kansas City, when Nebraska recruited him. Warren was a senior on the 1962 team, and I remember he fumbled the ball the first two times he got in our first game against South Dakota that year. He had been mostly a defensive player as a sophomore and junior, but we used him at both left halfback and fullback. He was a good blocker. He said his goal was for us to score on Missouri, his home state, that year. In the four years Danny Devine had been there, Nebraska hadn't scored a point on Missouri. We scored on them, but we lost the game 16-7. That was one of two we lost in our first year at Nebraska.

This time I presented an award to someone else, Nebraska Gov. Norbert Tiemann.

Warren, Dwain Carlson and Dennis Stuewe all played for me on the Blue squad in the Blue-Gray game at Montgomery, Alabama, after that season, and Warren went on to become a great pro player for the Oakland Raiders. He played six or seven years in the pros and started in a Super Bowl game against the Green Bay Packers. Warren lasted about seven minutes before he was knocked unconscious. I don't think he ever got back in the game, which the Packers won. Warren used to remind people that the score was 0-0 when he left the game. He also said he was the highest paid Oakland starter in that game, which meant he got paid about $1,000 a minute for the seven minutes he played. The next year he became an assistant for us.

Another story people used to tell about Warren, they said he was the individual most responsible for the Buffalo Bills getting O.J. Simpson when they drafted him out of Southern California. When Simpson was a senior in college, the Bills had a terrible team. All their quarterbacks got hurt and they finished the season with a split end playing quarterback. In the last game of the season, Buffalo was playing Oakland, and Oakland had already earned a spot in the playoffs, so the Raiders weren't very enthused about playing the game. Late in the game, Buffalo had the football down inside the Oakland one-yard line and if the Bills could have scored they'd have won the ball game. So this quarterback, the split end, rolled out on an option. Warren was playing in the Oakland secondary, and he figured the guy wasn't about to pass so he charged up and made a real hard hit. He jarred the ball loose behind the line of scrimmage, and it came down about a foot or so in-bounds. If the ball had gone out-of-bounds, Buffalo would have maintained possession and could still have won the football game. But Warren was still on his feet, and he reached out and grabbed the ball with one hand while keeping one foot in-bounds before he finally fell out-of-bounds. Buffalo lost the game and wound up in last place in the league, which meant the Bills got the first draft pick. If it hadn't been for

Warren, Buffalo wouldn't have finished last and wouldn't have been able to pick O.J. Simpson.

Warren left Nebraska and went to Washington State about the time Monte Kiffin was looking into the Oregon job. People said they might both end up in the Pac 8 Conference. They really liked Warren at Washington State. When he came back here and beat Nebraska, in their locker room after that game, their quarterback, Jack Thompson — a Samoan — stopped me and said: "I can't believe you ever let Warren Powers leave this place, but I want to personally thank you." I don't think he was trying to be a wise guy. They were just really happy with Warren. That was before he bought his way out of his contract and went to Missouri the next year. Jackie Sherrill was the coach at Washington State before Warren, and he had signed a long-term contract, too. Then Sherrill left right away for Pittsburgh, where they had just won a national championship. You can't really blame him for that, but those people up in Pullman, Washington, were getting a little skeptical, just like the people in Wyoming were worried that their program was becoming a stepping stone for ambitious young coaches. When Warren went up to interview, the people at Washington State asked him if he'd consider leaving if the Nebraska job suddenly opened up. Naturally, he said, "No."

Warren was from Kansas City and his wife was from St. Louis, so I guess you can't blame him too much. He told them he should have read the fine print in his contract. Then someone pointed out that the part about not becoming a head coach at some other school was in the same size print as the rest of it. I had to laugh a little bit; when Warren first got to Columbia, some newspaper story said that in his first year as a head coach, Warren Powers had taken Washington State to the Rose Bowl. The writer had gotten it wrong; it was Washington, not Washington State, that went to the Rose Bowl. Warren's first team was 6-5. Missouri earned bowl invitations the first year three years Warren was there. He's done a good job as a head coach.

chapter thirteen

*But Coach,
I want to carry
the football*

We never really had any serious racial problems at Nebraska. I remember one time Dick Davis, who was a very articulate young man and very concerned about individual rights, called a meeting of the black athletes and the coaching staff to talk about some things. Dick was academic All-Big Eight and got some mention for academic All-American as I recall. He was also quite an artist, and he drew caricatures of all the coaches for our football news media guide in 1968. Anyway, he was kind of the guy in charge, and he got up in the meeting and said to the other black athletes: "Well, what are some things we're concerned about?" He was grasping a little bit, I think. The only two complaints I can remember were, some of the black football players didn't think they were getting a fair shake on finding jobs over the summer, and then Dick brought up the fact that Joe Orduna was carrying the football too much and he was getting tired. Dick said we were giving the ball to Joe too often.

I said: "All right, I won't have Orduna carry the ball so much anymore."

After the meeting, Joe came up and said: "But Coach, I want to carry the football."

We had another meeting of all the black athletes over in the basement of the Coliseum, where they went over a lot of things, and again, they didn't have any real serious complaints. It all seemed pretty good-natured. It certainly wasn't a hostile meeting, not at all. That's the meeting where one of the black basketball players said: "I've been on the basketball team for two years, and one of the coaches still calls me 'Sherwin Jarmon.' Do we all look alike or something?"

I said, "Of course not."

"Well, that coach sure thinks I'm Sherwin."

That brought the house down, and I said, "Well, Sherwin's mad, too. He doesn't like it either."

Sherwin was a fine defensive end who came from Pershing High School in Detroit. I know he came from a tough neighborhood. He's one guy who maybe didn't get all the recognition he should have gotten, he and Mike Wynn. Wynn was a defensive end from Evanston, Illinois, the same high school that Bob Pickens came from — I'll tell you a funny story about him a little later. I think Sherwin might have been a little more mobile than Mike, but they were both good ones. I don't think Sherwin was probably as good as Jimmy Williams; he wasn't a Williams-type player, nothing like that, but he was better than most defensive ends we've had here. He was a great clutch player. You could always count on Sherwin to come up with the big plays when you needed them, but he probably didn't have the speed to be a really great player like Williams.

Anyway, it was during that meeting that Leroy Chalk, a basketball player, fell asleep. Clete Fischer looked over at him, tapped him on the shoulder, and said: "Leroy, you'd better wake up. We might need your vote." The meetings all ended up being more funny than serious. I guess I wasn't expecting a revolt or anything. I think they were partly a result of our having a couple of unsatisfactory seasons; this all happened back in 1967 or 1968. And you've got to remember, these things were happening all over the country at that time.

These players were about half apologetic about things. They were never belligerent, I know that, and I suspect they might have been getting some outside pressure. Dick Davis wasn't necessarily the leader, but he was one of the more prominent football players at the time, and he was a very intelligent guy. Dick was an All-Big Eight fullback. Sherwin Jarman was in there, of course, and Mike Wynn and Joe Orduna were concerned.

As you know, I grew up and worked in the foundries in Saginaw, Michigan, where black guys and white guys worked side-by-side. Black or white, there was no difference as far as I was concerned. There was never any other way of looking at people as far as I knew, and working in the foundry and living in Saginaw helped me in my outlook toward people right from the beginning. At Michigan State, where I started as a college coach, many of our greatest athletes were black. LeRoy Bolden and Clarence Peaks were two of the best ever. LeRoy Bolden was probably the best athlete, or at least the best football player certainly, I ever saw at Michigan State. The teams he played on there were tough. I think when LeRoy was a kid he got involved in a fight in which a guy was killed. LeRoy had seen some tough times, but he was a good person and a great football player.

We had a lot of black players at Michigan State, but I don't think Wyoming ever had a black player until we recruited Mike Walker out of Michigan. I'm pretty sure Mike was the first black football player, and maybe the first black athlete, Wyoming ever had. Walker came from Detroit. We laid the groundwork and brought him out to Laramie. We got him a place to stay, and it was never a big problem that I can remember, even though it was something we did a lot of thinking about before deciding to do it. We didn't want Mike to get all the way to Wyoming and then feel uncomfortable or out-of-place. Mike was a fine football player, and as a sophomore he helped us tie for the Skyline Conference championship. He was a chunky, hard-running back who single-handedly carried us his sophomore season; Mike was our left halfback. Chuck Lamson, a transfer from Iowa State, was our quarterback that year, but Chuck was hurt a lot and didn't play all that much, so Mike Walker had to carry more than his share of the load.

That was 1961, the season we went to Lawrence, Kansas, and tied the Kansas team with John Hadl, Curtis McClinton and some other great players.

Mike Walker had a tragic thing happen to him when he was a junior. I don't know where Mike is now; I don't think he went back to Detroit, but I know he never graduated from Wyoming. The year after we left Wyoming, Mike was sitting in a dorm room with Dave Marion, another black player, from Bakersfield, Calif. Marion was the finest punter I've ever seen kick the football. Mike and Dave and some other players were fooling around after the season, and they had a revolver in the room. Mike pointed the gun at Marion, and Dave told him to go ahead and pull the trigger. No one thought the gun was loaded, but it was. The gun went off, and the bullet hit Marion in the neck and severed his spinal cord enough so that he was never the same during the rest of his life. Marion died a few years later. That finished Mike Walker; he didn't play another down of football at Wyoming. It was a very tragic situation.

Getting back to black athletes, we were kind of pioneers in bringing them out to Wyoming's football program, and when we came to Nebraska, we went back into Michigan and Ohio and recruited heavily there. Right away we got guys like Freeman White, who was from Detroit, Tony Jeter, Harry Wilson, and a big tackle, Jerry Patton, from Saginaw, Michigan, my old stomping ground. Jeter was from Weirton, West Virginia, and Wilson, "Light Horse" they called him, was from Steubenville, Ohio. I remember when Harry first got here, some guy interviewed him on

television. He said: "Harry, you're a good open-field runner, and all, but what happens when they corner you?"

Harry said: "I don't know. I've never been cornered."

He used to walk around campus wearing a letter jacket
that had so many letters and medals and award stuff on it
that it's a wonder he could move.

Wilson had a promising career in the pros with the Philadelphia Eagles until he tore an achilles tendon twice and
had a knee injury. He had four frustrating years there,
then got involved with the wrong crowd. He was on probation for a couple of years, but now he's a foreman on a labor
force for Gulf Oil Company in Philadelphia. Finally, things
are going well for Harry once again.

Wilson was on the team that played in the 1964 Orange
Bowl against Auburn. After that game we wound up being
rated fifth in the nation, and that was the first Top 10 finish for Nebraska in a long time. That was also a landmark
game in another respect because it was the first time that
Auburn had ever played against a team that had any black
players. There were no incidents or anything like that on
the field; the game was conducted in a very sportsmanlike
manner. When we arrived in Miami prior to the game to
make arrangements for a place for our team to stay, the Orange Bowl people took us to this one hotel, the Ivanhoe.
We got to know the manager real well later on, because we
stayed at the Ivanhoe many times. They had just finished
remodeling it then. When they asked, we told them we had
some black players, and this manager hesitated a minute
and then he said: "That's no problem."

But then, just before we went down to Miami to start
preparing for the Orange Bowl, someone from the hotel
called us and wanted to know if we could keep the black
players out of the lobby and get them to go down to the
beach and swim instead of them hanging around and swimming in the hotel pool. I said: "Hell no, we're not going to
do that." The manager didn't care; actually, he was great
about it, but he had some regular guests who stayed there
every winter, who heard we were coming to stay in the

All-American end Freeman White.

hotel. They were the ones who tried to raise a big stink. After the game, though, the black players had a special party. They didn't go to the one the Orange Bowl put on for our football team.

Fortunately, we've come a long way in this country since then. But really, when you think about it, that wasn't so long ago. The first time we played down in Oklahoma in 1962, we had a problem like that. After the game, which was the last one of the season, Mike Corgan said to Bill Thornton: "Come on, I'll buy you a beer." So they went into a bar in Oklahoma City, and the bartender wouldn't serve Bill. Mike got madder 'en hell, but Bill just said to forget it and they went somewhere else.

When we came to Nebraska, I think we recruited more black players than they had ever recruited here before. Of course, there were some good ones already here, guys like Willie Ross, Rudy Johnson, Tyrone Robertson, and Bill Thornton.

While I'm talking about some of our black players, I might mention Ben Gregory, who was one of the best all-around football players we ever had at Nebraska. Ben was more popular with his teammates than Johnny Rodgers, and he was probably just as good of a football player as Rodgers; he just didn't play on the same kinds of teams. When Rodgers was here, we were fortunate enough to have people who could get him the football, guys like Tagge, Brownson and Humm. That wasn't always true with Gregory.

He was from Uniontown, Pennsylvania, and he's a cousin to Gene Huey, who coaches our wingbacks and tight ends now. Ben could throw the football; he could catch the ball; he could run with it, and he could play defense. He was an excellent defensive player, and we used him on occasion on defense, even when we were a two-platoon football team and he was mainly playing offense. There wasn't anything Ben couldn't do. He went into pro football and had problems with one of his knees. Ben Gregory was a regular right away with the Buffalo Bills; he was good, a sure-fire pro player and a star. But after the first year, his one knee had gotten really torn up. It was about as bad as the doctors had ever seen. Ben went to Colorado and is teaching school there now. He's getting along real well.

Ben played as a sophomore on the 1965 team. He was Harry Wilson's back-up, and he had a good day in the Orange Bowl against Alabama, even though we lost the game. He caught a 49-yard touchdown pass from Bob Churchich in that game. Gregory started out on defense his junior year but when Ron Kirkland got hurt, we switched Ben to that halfback spot. I checked the records and in his senior year, Gregory completed three passes, caught 14 and rushed for over 400 yards. He had a great day here in Lincoln in that last game against Oklahoma. He did a little bit of everything for us. Gregory was an outstanding player and a fine person.

I mentioned Bob Pickens earlier. He transferred to Nebraska from Wisconsin and went on to play professional football with the Chicago Bears, near his home in Evanston, Illinois. Bob was a tackle, and he was big, about 6-5 and over 270 pounds. Bob was on the 1966 team that played in the Sugar Bowl and lost to Alabama, 34-7; so was Gregory. We were 9-0 and ranked fourth in the nation when we went down to Oklahoma for the last game of the season. They beat us 10-9 when a guy named Vachon kicked a field goal with 48 seconds left. What an afternoon. We had guys dropping the ball when it was right in their hands. On one play, we ran to our left to throw a pass. Oklahoma had a big crest on its field, and the quarterback sailed the ball way over the fullback's head; he was all alone in the end zone. We did so many bad things in that game.

Once again we weren't playing for the Big Eight championship though, because we already had it clinched, and I think that hurt us. That hurt us a couple of times against Oklahoma because the same intensity and the same incentive are missing under the circumstances. We should have won that game, probably more so than any game Nebraska has ever lost to Oklahoma.

So anyway, off we went to the Sugar Bowl to play a very good Alabama team that included Kenny Stabler. I remember before the game I told Kaye Carstens, who was a fine defensive back, to watch out early in the game that they didn't fake to the fullback and hit Ray Perkins, their real good receiver, going down the sidelines. Well, sure enough, they received the kickoff and ran it back to about the 22-yard line. On the first play of the game, Stabler faked to the fullback going into the line and hit Perkins down field. Perkins caught it running full speed, and we couldn't catch him until he had gotten inside our 30-yard line. Carstens was following my instructions, all right. He was watching . . . watching Perkins run down the field.

But getting back to Pickens, we got off to a bad start in that Sugar Bowl game, right away, before the opening kick-off, in fact. We were in the locker room getting ready to go out on the field, and Pickens wanted to know if he could say a few words to the team. He wanted to get everyone fired up. So he got up and said, emotional-like: "Let's dedicate this game to the three guys who got killed in the airplane crash coming down here." It was three alums flying a private plane down to the game. Everyone just looked at each other without saying anything. None of the players knew those three guys from Adam. My God, when we went out of the locker room, our goal was to win the game for three guys nobody had ever heard of. It wasn't quite like trying to win one for the Gipper.

I'll also never forget before that game one of the television guys asked me if we could win. I told him: "We'll have to play our best game of the year and Alabama will have to play its worst game of the year or they're going to win." The score tells what happened. They had so much speed, we couldn't stay with them. We were pretty big and slow that year. It was after that game that I decided we needed more speed, so we recruited some smaller players the next year. The only trouble was, they also turned out to be slower, and that led to the problems we had in 1967 and 1968, when we had the 6-4 seasons back-to-back.

Langston Coleman was a pretty well-known black player who came here as a walk-on from Washington, D.C. He had a big scar on his face, a distinctive mark which made him immediately recognizable to everyone. He hitch-hiked here to visit with another tough kid who decided not to enroll, but anyway, we didn't know much about either one of them. Langston turned out to be a great player for us. He and Jerry Murtaugh were a couple of the meanest football players we ever had at Nebraska. Coleman was about as nasty in practice hitting people as anybody could be. During practice the other players used to hate being in drills with Langston because he'd beat the heck out of guys in what we called a "dummy drill." They were glad when game day arrived so they wouldn't have to line up against him. Langston was a tough guy, all right. Once before a game, he stood up and said: "Today, we take no prisoners." You could tell he meant it. He taught school for awhile in Wisconsin and now he's a lobbyist for the United States Conference of Mayors in Washington, D.C. Langston Coleman is one of the best friends I ever made among my former players. We still keep in touch.

chapter fourteen

*Going to a bowl game
almost every year
helps in recruiting*

Recruiting is a fickle business. You never know what it is that causes a 17-year-old kid who is highly sought after by a number of colleges to pick one over the others.

Nebraska always starts out at a disadvantage because of the lack of population in the immediate area. Southern Cal has millions of people right in its own back yard. We had to interest a kid in coming hundreds, if not thousands, of miles from his home to order to play for the Huskers.

One thing that has made recruiting easier since I've been at Nebraska is the liklihood that the team will get to go to a post-season bowl game. That's a reward the players like.

From the time Nebraska started football in 1890 through the 1961 season — before I came to Lincoln — Nebraska had only been to two bowl games. There was, of course, the still-talked-about Rose Bowl game after the 1940 season. Incidentally, I had been at Nebraska for five years before I found out the Huskers lost that game to Stanford. The other bowl game was an Orange Bowl invitation following the 1954 season, which resulted in a 34-7 loss to Duke.

Not that we registered a victory every time out, but we managed to make it to nine bowl games in the 11 years I was the head coach at Nebraska. We won six of the nine. In addition, Tom has had a team in a bowl game every year since he took over. That record has been valuable in recruiting.

Winning the two back-to-back national championships in 1970 and '71 and getting ranked in the Top Ten every year — Nebraska has been in a national wire service Top Ten every year since 1970 — has also helped recruiting greatly.

Going to a bowl game our first season — and winning such an exciting game, 36-34, over a good team like Miami of Florida, which had such a great passer in George Mira — really got things going for us. We followed in 1963 with our first Big Eight championship and that launched the string of major bowl appearances that has continued pretty much without interruption ever since.

It wasn't as though I didn't have any material when I arrived at Nebraska in 1962. I inherited a good group of juniors. And speaking of the material I inherited, at banquets I often enjoy telling the story — even if it isn't true — about the circumstances surrounding Coach Bill Jennings being let out, although he had some good players coming back.

When I first arrived in Lincoln I was invited to a meeting of the Touchdown Club. To my surprise, they also invited Jennings, even though he had already been fired. And it was the Touchdown Club members who had been very instrumental in getting him fired.

Well, during the course of the program they asked Jennings if he would like to say a few words. I was surprised as hell, but Jennings said, "Yes," he would.

He got up in front of this group that had cost him his job

and said, "I'm not going to say 'goodbye' because that's too final. I'm not going to say 'so long' because I really don't care if I see any of you again. I'm not going to say 'Hasta la vista' or 'Auf Wiedersehen' or 'Arrivederci' because I don't think there are many of you who would know what I'm talking about. But as I go out the yonder door, I would like you to note carefully the sprig of mistletoe that I have attached to my coat tail." This wasn't true, but it's a good story.

When I first took over, we brought in what we thought were some pretty good football players that first year, although we had a little trouble selling them on coming to Nebraska. We used some connections we had back in some areas where I had recruited when I was at Michigan State and again after moving to Wyoming. Then the next year, after winning the Gotham Bowl, recruiting became a little easier. There wasn't any limit on the number of scholarships we could give at that time. Then they came down to a limit of 45 a few years later.

We recruited heavily in the Big Ten area. The Big Ten had a "need" clause and more restrictive scholastic requirements than we did. All of that helped us get started.

Each coach recruited a different area. John Melton took Pennsylvania. Jim Ross and Mike Corgan worked Michigan, where they had been high school coaches. Carl Selmer had Minnesota and Iowa. Clete Fischer worked the state of Nebraska and George Kelly went up in the Green Bay area and Chicago.

We didn't have a recruiting coordinator like they do now. And Tom didn't do much recruiting that first year or two. He was still a professor and was working on his doctor's degree.

We thought we had our staff all set when Tom first showed up. He said he had decided not to play pro football any more, that he wanted to go to school, work on his doctorate and wanted to help us coach. I said, "Fine, but we don't have any money in the budget for another coach." He

After the Gotham Bowl. Nebraska 36, Miami 34. The first of nine bowls for my Husker teams.

said that didn't matter, he just wanted to get involved in coaching. And so he coached that first year for nothing. I think about all he got was a few free meals at the training table.

We had a good nucleus for our second season in 1963 and we figured we had a good shot at the Big Eight championship. We wound up having some close ball games. One of the closest was down at Missouri. They got ahead of us, but we regained the lead. Later, they scored and went for two points. Bruce Smith broke up the two-point try in the end zone and we beat them, 13-12.

Of course the game that stands out the biggest that year was our early loss to Air Force. In that game we realized that the Nebraska fans would not accept defeat. They had become accustomed — even at that early stage — to being a winner. We got a tremendous amount of criticism — justified, I'd have to admit — for losing that ball game.

We had a bigger team and there was no reason the Air Force should have beaten us. They got away with a couple of long passes. It was a real fiasco. We didn't play well on offense and had a couple of defensive lapses. Air Force came up on that one occasion with a very inspired performance. I always felt, however, that game was sort of a catalyst to help us go on the rest of the way.

That game kinda woke people up. We were criticized by the news media. I remember the papers at the time were very critical. And rightfully so. It made me realize that I wasn't home free, despite having had such a good first season.

As that '63 season went along, we had some other close games besides the one with Missouri. Then, in the final game for the championship, we played Oklahoma in Lincoln. The big story of that game was that it followed by just a day the time that President Kennedy had been shot. There was a big question as to whether the game would be played or not.

Oklahoma Coach Bud Wilkinson came up with the statement that settled the issue. He had been closely associated with Kennedy. And Bud said he was sure that the President would have wanted the game to be played. The assassination happened around noon on Friday. We were up all that night. At first, I really didn't think about any affect it would have on the football game. Then I started hearing where other schools were going to cancel their games. Then it came to the point where maybe our game would be called off. I think it was Bud's statement that changed the thinking. He talked to Bobby Kennedy, who encouraged us to go ahead with the game.

I think that was one of only a few major college games to be played that day. There certainly weren't many. We received some mild criticism for it, but it was outweighed by the fact we won our first Big Eight championship.

A lot of schools had said they were going to play, so we assumed we would too. Then, most of the others changed their minds at the last minute. The final decision on our game wasn't made until about 10 minutes before the kickoff of a nationally televised game. The other two Big Eight games that were scheduled that day were canceled at the very last minute. We wanted to play. After all, we thought we had a good chance to win it. To cancel it would have screwed up the Orange Bowl situation.

I don't think the shooting of the president affected the outcome of the game or the players. The players were concerned — as all of us were. But once the game got started, I don't think it entered the players' minds. As coaches, once the game was under way, there was no thought about anything except the action on the field.

Our players went both ways — offense and defense — in 1962 and '63. Two-platoon football didn't come in until a year after that. It was probably helpful to our coaching staff to have single-platoon rules when we first came to Nebraska. We didn't have to recruit as many good players to get things going. I was always for two-platoon — and I still am.

We changed to a two-platoon system just before the Minnesota game of 1964. We played South Dakota in our

Claridge, Brown and Voss went with me to the All-American game in Lubbock in June of 1964.

opening game and beat them, 56-0, with a single-platoon team. I don't know whether the rules weren't changed yet or whether we just didn't want Minnesota to know what we were going to do. I suspect it was the latter.

When we had to make the decisions on dividing the squad, we put Jeter and White and most of the good players on offense. I don't know if that was the right decision or not. A lot of teams today load up the defense. But we had a helluva game up there against Minnesota. We beat them 26-21. That was the game where their linebacker tipped the pass in the end zone into Kent McCloughan's hands for the deciding touchdown.

As I said earlier, probably the best two-way player I coached during those first two years was Bob Brown. He was a good linebacker and a fine offensive guard.

Larry Kramer was another great two-way player. We probably made a mistake when we went offense-defense with him, however. We put Larry on offense. He made all-American as an offensive tackle, but he was probably a better defensive player.

Bill Thornton was another. He backed up the line in addition to being a great ball carrier. And Ben Gregory, Warren Powers and Kent McCloughan. Most of the players we had were good all-around football players. Dwain Carlson and John Kirby were two more. Kirby played several years as a linebacker for the Vikings. Yet he was an offensive guard for us. I've likely left out some others who also should be mentioned. I don't mean to overlook anybody. But that was nearly 20 years ago.

chapter fifteen

*The pressure of recruiting
was one of the reasons
I quit coaching*

Another great two-way player we had at Nebraska when we made the switch to two-platoon football was Tony Jeter. I'll never forget recruiting him. Jim Ross was the assistant coach most closely in touch with Tony and his family, but Jim thought I ought to go talk to them, too. He told me about Mrs. Jeter. He said she played the organ for the choir at her church, and Jim told me it would really impress her if I would offer to sit down and sing some hymns with her. Well, sure enough, when I called at their home, she invited me to sit down on the organ bench alongside her. But, after one or two pieces, she'd had enough of my singing.

I liked recruiting in those early years. But, eventually, the pressure of recruiting was one of the things that led me to hang it up as a coach. Once you got to where the kid was and sat down to visit with him and his parents, I didn't mind that. In fact, I liked that part of recruiting. But the constant traveling, the scrambling to get from one place to another, that was tough.

Some of the things that happened when I was out recruiting were pretty funny. I remember when I was an assistant at Michigan State I was back in Pittsburgh where we were after this Greek kid. So were Indiana, Illinois and Purdue. The Big Ten had a rule at that time that you weren't allowed to visit a kid in his home, but I went out to his house anyway. When I got there, one of those other coaches was in the house and the other two were standing on the porch. We were all in violation, although today that wouldn't be a violation. You run into a lot of crazy situations like this in recruiting.

Duffy Daugherty was the head coach at Michigan State then. When I first was hired as an assistant there, Biggie Munn was the head coach and Duffy was his chief assistant. Duffy wanted me to bring the Greek kid out to Michigan State. He had me borrow a car from a car dealer in Pittsburgh. So I borrowed the car and started the trip with the kid and his mother and father. I'm telling you, it was hot as hell, and we didn't have any air conditioning. The mother must have weighed 260 pounds, and the little Greek dad was about 5-foot-5. The mother was giving the dad hell all the time, and she'd keep saying to the kid, "Say something, say something." We rode in that damn car all the way from Pittsburgh to Lansing. I was never so glad to get anyplace in all my life.

Another time, in Chicago, we were trying to get the kids of a couple of policemen. I was up in a hotel room drinking with these two cops. It was hot as the dickens that day, too, and the room didn't have air conditioning. One of the cops took off his pants and he had on these wild shorts with Christmas tree ornaments all over them. After while, their wives arrived. The other cop's wife took one look and said, "Look at the balls on that guy!" There were hundreds of funny things that happened while recruiting.

I was back recruiting in Boston one time for Michigan State. We were after two brothers — the McNeelys. Tom was the main one. He later fought Floyd Patterson for the heavyweight championship. Brian was his brother. They were supposedly good football players although we hadn't seen any film on them. Their dad was a great old Irishman. You'd get in the house and the first thing the father would do is set a bottle down on the table. Before you'd talk about anything else, you'd have to have a couple of drinks with him. Another Big Ten coach was also after the McNeely brothers. Now Mr. NcNeely was a great guy, but he was also looking for the best situation for his sons. While it wasn't legal to give money to the players, you could get them jobs. In some cases, the job didn't require much work.

Mr. McNeely would call up Duffy and say, "Duffy, I just got a call from the other coach. He says he'll give each of the kids a $75 a month job instead of the $50 jobs you were talking about." Duffy would then call me. "Tell them we'll go 75 bucks also." Then, a little while later, the dad would call and say, "Duffy, that other coach just says he'll find them $100 a month jobs." Well, finally, we got the McNeelys for $100 jobs each.

All the McNeelys came out to visit the campus. Duffy takes them over to eat at Schuler's Restaurant in Marshall, about 20 miles away. This was a great place to eat, known all over the world. We get in the car and start the drive. Phyllis was in the car, along with Duffy and his wife, and Mr. and Mrs. McNeely, six of us in a car that wasn't all that big, and McNeely says, "If you go to school here do you have to go this far everytime you want to eat?" You remember things like that.

Incidentally, neither of the McNeely kids turned out to be very good football players, although Tom was a good boxer. Brian used to do his fighting in the bars — and he won most of his fights.

The McNeelys were wonderful people and even though Tom and Brian left Michigan State, we remained good friends. When I was at Wyoming later, I'd stay with the McNeelys when I was in the Boston area and they'd help me recruit.

Speaking of recruiting at Wyoming, after I got my first

Tony Jeter signed his pro contract with the Green Bay Packers immediately after the 1966 Orange Bowl game.

head coaching job, because of our limited recruiting budget
we would drive rather than fly. To save money we would
sometimes disconnect the speedometer to cut down on the
mileage cost. We also would stay in some pretty bad motels
and also eat at the cheapest possible joints.

We needed extra recruiters when we were at Wyoming.
Not to recruit the kids, but to keep them in Laramie once
we got them. We had to keep one coach at the bus depot,
one at the airport and another at the train station to keep
our players from leaving town. One of our best recruiters —
then and now — was John Melton. He can go in and talk to
any family. He can mix in with any type of person easily. If
they want to talk nice, he can do that. If they want to get
down and talk some other way he can do that, too. And
he's funnier than hell; he'll get 'em laughing and break the
ice real easily.

I remember one of the big recruiting projects John and I
worked together on after we got to Nebraska was over Rich
Costanzo from Jersey City. I went in there to help out.
Rich lived on a real dark street. I was about half scared
going down those streets at night in Jersey City. We took
Costanzo, his mother and father, his sister and her boy-
friend — there were eight or 10 of us — to this Italian restaurant. They ordered wine, the works. We had an Italian
dinner that cost over $150. That's for food that usually
isn't all that expensive anyway, and, besides, that was a
long time ago, when things were a lot less expensive. They
were nice people, but it's a good thing, with today's prices,
that it's illegal to entertain like that any more. Our athletic
budget would really be in the red.

Recruiting David Humm out of Las Vegas was another
interesting case. Everybody was after Dave Humm. The
parents, his father Claire and mother Anne, were really
nice people. Claire was a cashier at Caesar's Palace. Alabama was our biggest competition for Dave. Alabama re-
portedly had some real nice-looking girl lined up for Dave.
But, of course, good-looking girls in Las Vegas are almost a
drug on the market. Anyway, Dave never had any trouble

when it came to good-looking girls. He never needed any outside help.

We had a guy who was on our side. His name was Marvin Sillman, and he's the one who eventually got Dave Humm to come to Nebraska. I had known Marvin for years. He ran the baccarat game at Caesar's. Marvin was a really nice person. He came from Buffalo, New York, and had been a gambler all his life. Dave Humm's dad had confidence in what Marvin Sillman thought. I told Marv what we'd do for the kid. We didn't offer him one single thing that was illegal, and Sillman told Dave's dad, "You can believe these people from Nebraska. They'll do right for Dave." That was it. That got him for us. Without Marvin Sillman, Dave Humm would have probably been playing for Alabama or some other school.

John Melton and I both would like to take credit for successfully recruiting Dave Humm. We both worked hard and sort of enjoyed recruiting in Las Vegas. But without the help of Marvin Sillman, I doubt if we'd have gotten the job done.

One of the few times we got investigated by the NCAA, while I was coaching at Nebraska, was over Dave Humm. He was still in high school at the time, but came down to our Sun Bowl game against Georgia in El Paso following the 1969 season. He came down there on his own. We didn't pay his way or anything, but he did have a couple of meals with us and we took him out to practice with us on the team bus. It seemed pretty minor to me, but we got reprimanded for it.

The funny story on us recruiting Humm is that after we explained to him that he would get: "your room, your board, your tuition, your books and your laundry," John Melton paused and then laughingly added, "And the laundry will net you about $500 a month."

Speaking of recruiting a quarterback, it was interesting when we went after Tagge and Brownson the same year. We had a difficult time getting them both. Tagge was all right, but I spent a lot of time talking to the Brownsons and trying to convince them that their kid was gonna be our quarterback. They knew I was also recruiting Tagge.

And they also knew we were recruiting Max Linder, the quarterback from Plattsmouth. And actually, when they were all freshmen, Tagge was third. Linder and Brownson were the top two quarterbacks. But Max never really was in the fight after that freshman year. He kind of fell by the wayside for various reasons.

Brownson was a very sought-after high school quarterback. And Tagge was up there too. Henry Atkinson helped us a great deal in recruiting Tagge and other players from Green Bay. We got Jimmy Anderson and Tagge the same year. And we got Dave Mason a year later. And we had Dennis Gutzman the year before. They were all good football players.

With the Brownsons, we just convinced them that Nebraska was the right distance from home and we were playing better football than any of the other teams recruiting him. We had Mr. and Mrs. Brownson over here and we had Van playing golf and we tried every way we could to convince him. I probably worked as hard on Brownson as any kid. Brownson and Humm. Tagge too, but we had some more help on him.

We also started recruiting in California for the first time. We got a great bunch that very first year — Bob Newton, Dick Rupert and Keith Wortman. We brought them back to Nebraska one weekend when it was the worst weather you could imagine. We thought, "This is crazy. We'll never see these guys again." But they all came to school in Lincoln. For the next few years we got some great players from California.

Bob Terrio was also among the first Californians we got. He intercepted a pass right at the end of the 1970 national championship game against LSU. After I quit coaching, I think Tom Osborne had about 14 kids from California on the squad at one time. We started working California at the end of the 1968 season. That was about the time we had fallen down quite a lot in our recruiting. Our main

John Melton and I sign David Humm while his family watches.

problem was the failure to recruit a good quarterback. We had recruited Frank Patrick from Derry, Pennsylvania. He was going to be our savior. Frank was a 6-7 passer — but he never really worked out, never lived up to our expectations, so we had to go to Ernie Sigler, a guy with a great heart but not too much of an arm. We scrambled there for a couple of years. Frank had that one great game against Oklahoma, where he passed for 267 yards and set a Big Eight record. That was by far his best game. He certainly had some ability. After all, he stayed with the Green Bay Packers for three or four years as their backup quarterback. He finished here at Nebraska as a tight end. One thing about Frank, wherever he played he gave us 100 percent at all times.

One problem Frank had at quarterback was that his delivery of the ball was awfully hard. And Frank didn't read defenses real quick. I guess it was a combination of things. He'd have a hot streak and then he couldn't hit anything. Maybe if we'd have been playing a different kind of offense, spending more time passing, Frank would have been a better passer and more valuable to us, but he couldn't run very much. The only time we lost to Colorado in 20 years was when he threw a couple of interceptions which they ran way back, but I have to take a lot of the blame for that loss. I called a fourth-down quarterback sneak when we were ahead, 7-0, on our own 25-yard line. It was one of the poorest calls I ever made. But I figured a guy 6-foot-7 inches tall could fall forward far enough for a first down. And he did. Only thing was, he forgot the ball.

chapter sixteen

*Coaching the Shrine
and pro all-star games
brings back memories*

During my years at Nebraska, I was invited to be a part of the coaching staff for several all-star games. I was in Hawaii for the Hula Bowl a couple of times and also involved in the All-American game in Lubbock and the North-South Shrine game in Miami.

The two which were probably the most interesting were the East-West Shrine game in San Francisco and the College-Pro All Star game which used to be played every summer in Chicago. I was the head coach for both of those games. I coached the West team in the Shrine Bowl after the 1968 season and the college team against the pros the summer after our second straight national championship — the summer of '72. The next fall was my last season of coaching. That game was especially memorable because the Nebraska coaching staff was the all-star staff as a unit. Our whole group was there. Also, five Nebraska seniors from the '71 team were chosen on the College All-Star roster —

Jerry Tagge, Jeff Kinney, Larry Jacobson, Bob Terrio and Van Brownson. Dick Rupert was brought in later, when we had an injury on the squad, and he played in the game, too. In fact, Dick found himself playing right across the line from Bob Lilly of the Cowboys. That was quite an experience, especially since Rupert was giving away about 50 pounds.

Winning the East-West Shrine game turned out to be especially satisfying because I had just come off those two 6-4 seasons at Nebraska. Besides, the coaches for the East team — John Pont, Duffy Daugherty and Tom Cahill had all been selected as Coach of the Year at one time or another. And they had guys like Ed Podolak from Iowa and Mike Phipps from Purdue. Supposedly, they had the top bunch of football players.

Our West squad — Dee Andros from Oregon State and Don Coryell, who now coaches in the pros but was then at San Diego State, were the other coaches with me — was made up of lesser-known football players than probably any all star squad ever gathered. In fact, we didn't even have what you could call an established quarterback. We had Ronnie Johnson from Oklahoma State. I suppose we had another quarterback, but I don't remember who he was. Ronnie played most of the time.

But we did have some guys who were potentially pretty good. There was Joe Greene from North Texas State. But nobody had really heard much about "Mean Joe" at that time. And Freddie Dryer. What a wild man. And was he tough. He is still playing for the LA Rams. We also had Gene Washington, a fine receiver who played a lot of pro ball.

Gene Huey from Wyoming, who is now an assistant on Tom's staff at Nebraska, was the outstanding player of the game. I always thought Gene would be good in pro ball, but I guess he lacked a step of speed. Gene was a great athlete. And he's done a fine job for us at Nebraska since he came as an assistant coach. We could have signed Huey to a scholarship at Nebraska out of high school. He is Ben Gregory's cousin. But we didn't offer him. We thought he was too small. That was one of our all-time recruiting mistakes. He came back here with Wyoming and damn near beat us. And he turned in a great performance in that Shrine game.

When I got back to Lincoln after winning the game, I remember that Cliff Hardin said to me, "Well, you may have changed some people's opinion of you as a football coach. That East-West victory, beating all those Coach of the Year opponents, may have helped you more than you realize in the eyes of Nebraskans."

Actually, in 1967 we were just a short way off from being a pretty good football team. We started out by beating Washington out in Seattle. Then we beat Minnesota. The next week we ran our record to 3-0 by beating Kansas State. In that K-State game, Dennis Richnafsky set a Big Eight record by catching 14 passes.

Then things went sour for a couple of weeks. First we lost to Kansas, 10-0, down in Lawrence. I so badly underestimated Kansas. They'd lost three straight. They were not very good, but we played terrible.

Then we lost to Colorado. It was the only time I ever lost to Colorado. We should have won that one. But they ran two pass interceptions way back on us and beat us, 21-16.

We got back on track and beat TCU, Iowa State and Oklahoma State. So we were pretty respectable at 6-2. But we lost the last two, although we were barely beaten by Missouri, 10-7, and Oklahoma, 21-14.

It was a lot better 6-4 team than the record sounds. We could have beaten Oklahoma. We had a touchdown called back that day just before the half. Frank Patrick had his best day ever against Oklahoma, setting a new passing record.

The next year, in '68, we started out 3-0 again. Then everything went bad again. We got beat four times in the league, although none of the losses were by big scores except to Oklahoma. What made it worse is that we won three conference games on the road, but lost three of our home conference games, and then lost to Oklahoma in Norman to finish the season.

Walt Barnes and Freeman White as we headed to a Hula Bowl game.

The Kansas State game that year was Homecoming. I'll never forget it. They had a good passer, Lynn Dickey. He threw a long touchdown pass to Dave Jones the first time they got their hands on the ball, and that was all she wrote.

Chuck Fairbanks was the head coach at Oklahoma that year. We were just horrible that day, but I'll tell you something about Chuck. I coached him at Michigan State the last couple of years he was there. And I always felt that he didn't feel real great toward me because he didn't play much. When Chuck was a freshman, they were under the two-platoon rule. He was a very good offensive end, and he played quite a bit as a freshman. But then the players had to go both ways. He was poor on defense and didn't play much.

Well, in that '68 game, hell, he even put his best player, Steve Owens, back in the game to score their last touchdown. I thought Chuck might have been trying to get even with me. I didn't think that was a bit funny. But when he came over after the game, I just shook hands. I didn't say anything. That was definitely the lowest point of my coaching career.

That year, after a call from Phyllis, my secretary — her name was Dee Bykirk — threw all the bad letters away without me knowing it. She junked a lot of mail. I never did see all the really nasty letters where I was being called a bunch of bad names. If the letter was borderline and worth answering, she'd show it to me. I actually didn't realize how irritated the fans were.

But you know, even though we lost to Oklahoma both of those years, we generally played them pretty even. When it came to the Game of the Century in '71, they had won just one more game than we had in the series while I was the Nebraska coach.

But I have to admit that we blew two of those earlier Oklahoma games. We should have beaten them down there in 1964. And we should have won the 1966 game. We just played a couple of bad football games in losing those two.

In the '64 game they just took it to us. And this surprised the heck out of us. We didn't think they were going to be that good. They just ran right at us. And we weren't prepared to handle it.

So there were two — maybe even three games — where Oklahoma shouldn't have beaten us. The only times we felt Oklahoma was actually better than we were — when I was coaching — was the first year, 1962, and in 1967 and '68.

As I said earlier when discussing the '71 game, we actually felt we could defense Oklahoma much better than we did. And our offensive planning was sort of routine. It didn't include anything all that unusual. Of course, Rodgers ran a punt back for a touchdown. That really helped, and Kinney did a fine job carrying the ball. What probably made the game more exciting than it should have been was that we defensed Oklahoma much more poorly than we anticipated. We were a good offensive team, and we thought we could stop them.

The last drive of the game, where we controlled the ball and moved right down the field, showed the character and offensive strength of our ball club. I told Tagge, when he called time out during that drive, "As long as we can run the ball with Kinney, run. If you get in a problem, then try to hit Rodgers.

He kept feeding the ball to Kinney until we got in the one spot where we were third and about nine. So Jerry called perhaps the logical pass for that time. It was supposed to be an out pattern. He was going to throw to Rodgers on the outside. But Tagge got chased out of the pocket. Rodgers' pattern was broken because the timing was off on the play, so Johnny curled into the middle in kind of a deep hook. And Tagge hit him on the run. It wasn't a great throw, but Johnny dived and came up with the ball for a first down.

If we hadn't completed that pass, we'd have gone for it on fourth down. We didn't have time to kick and have any hope of getting the ball back again.

The way the game was going, the team that had the ball last was going to score and win the game. I was not as

An Orange Bowl queen between two thorns, Bob Newton and Jerry Murtaugh.

worried about that third-down pass being completed as I was later when Kinney fumbled the football near the goal line.

The refs called the ball dead. At the time, I have to admit, I thought we got a break. But the films showed that he was down before he fumbled. It was a good call, but it scared the hell out of me.

When that drive started I felt fairly confident that if we didn't make a mistake, we could go down and score. I don't remember being despondent, just because we were behind, or ever thinking that the game was lost. We had enough time, and I figured that if we kept moving the ball and didn't panic — that was the big thing — that we'd be okay. As you'll remember, Kinney carried the ball on every play of the drive except for the one pass to Rodgers. There was no reason to change. It was working.

Kinney was a strong runner and a tremendously determined runner. Jeff was very difficult to bring down. He would break tackles, he would slide tackles and he had disceptive speed. Jeff also had very good hands. He very seldom fumbled the ball or dropped a pass.

Jeff could also throw the ball — he was a high school quarterback in McCook. He was our best I-back during the years I coached because of his ability to run, throw and catch.

Since everybody knew he could throw it, if you pitched the ball out to Jeff, the defensive halfback couldn't come running right up because we'd send our wide receivers down field. Johnny Rodgers was on one side and Frosty Anderson on the other. That gave Jeff a little more time to maneuver to the outside.

Our 1971 team was good on offense, although Tom's team of a couple of years ago had better per-game statistics than our '71 national champs.

But the thing about the '71 team, that didn't show in the statistics, was Rodgers. We've never had a guy who was such a "big play" person.

Later, in the Orange Bowl, we were ahead of Alabama,

The Bear choked me in 1965, but I got him when it counted the most, by beating him for the national championship in the 1972 Orange Bowl.

28-0, at halftime. Oklahoma was leading Auburn, 31-0, at halftime in the Sugar Bowl. We were two very explosive football teams, certainly the two best in the country. I'm not sure Colorado should have been third in the final national ratings. Although Colorado beat Houston that year in the Bluebonnet Bowl.

I've wandered way off the subject. I was talking about the all-star games and never did really discuss the College-Pro game in Chicago.

I thought we had a good enough team to make a real run at the Dallas Cowboys. Although the college team seldom won in that series, we went into the game feeling we had a chance. Tagge didn't have one of his better days, however, and we had some misfortunes early in the game. We kicked off but stopped them in their first series, took over the ball and started right down the field, moving it real good. Then, all of a sudden, we got slapped with a 15-yard penalty and from that time on we didn't do much offensively until late in the game.

We had a lot of talent on that team. Franco Harris was one of our fullbacks, although he didn't play much. He was talking to his agent all the time instead of practicing. We used Bobby Newhouse, who was a draft choice of our opponent — Dallas — most of the time at fullback.

We had a great tight end in Riley Odoms. And we also had some great defensive backs — Willie Buchanan and Tommy Casanova — to name just two. There was one major problem. The defense had spent all its time preparing to play against Dallas's first-string quarterback, Roger Staubach. His style was rolling out, throwing on the run and scrambling. He was tough to contain. But he got hurt early in the game and the Cowboys brought in Craig Morton, who was a classic drop back passer.

That presented a different situation all together. Now you should be rushing the passer, blitzing, bringing people right straight in, not worrying about containment — like you did against Staubach.

Our defense just couldn't handle Morton. He's the guy

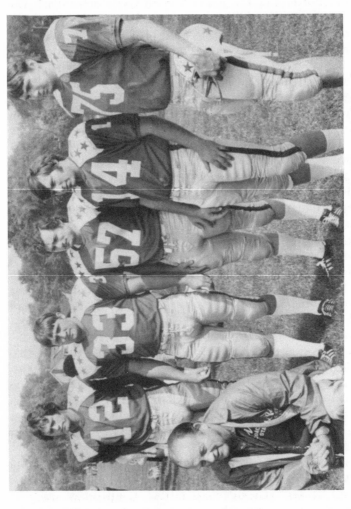

College All-Stars, 1972. Brownson, Kinney, Terrio, Tagge and Jacobson. Rupert was not in the picture, although he also played in the game.

who picked us apart. He did a good job of throwing the football, and we lost 20-7.

The sponsors of the game invited us to come back the next year, but I couldn't talk the whole staff into going again. Tom, who was getting ready to take over my job as the head coach at Nebraska, wanted them to be on hand that summer as he got ready for his first season, and I could certainly understand that. So, John McKay, who was at USC then, took the job coaching the all-stars.

Two years later the game was called in the second half because of a terrible rain storm. I think that was the last year for the game.

The pros didn't want or need it anymore. At one time, the pros wanted that game badly. It gave exposure to pro football, which was not big when that all star game was started. Later, it got so pro football was bigger than the game. That's when it was discontinued.

Speaking of that college-pro game, we stayed in this hotel in downtown Evanston. It was relatively close to Northwestern University, where we practiced. It wasn't a bad hotel, but it was not what you would call the best hotel. Anyway, there was a small bar in the hotel where most of the coaching staff would gather after practice for a pre-dinner drink or two.

George Kelly, who had been on my original staff at Nebraska and who was then an assistant at Notre Dame, came to visit us. One night after practice there were four or five coaches — including Kelly — in the bar area. We were at a table that was pushed right up to the wall. The waitress, when she brought a round of drinks, had to reach across to serve the guys on the far side.

She was a rather buxom young lady. We stayed in the bar longer than we had intended. One of the group, not George Kelly, couldn't resist the temptation and he pinched the waitress when she reached across the table. She jumped about a foot off the floor. The instant she came back on her feet, she whirled around and hit Kelly right across the chops — while the culprit was sitting there with a look of innocence. It's crazy how a thing like that will stick in your memory. But — at least at the time — it was really funny.

chapter seventeen

Great to see you,
but get on the other
side of the field

We tried to do little things to motivate our players before games, probably more so at Wyoming than at Nebraska. But we did some things here, too, like the time we let
Bob Pickens give his little speech before the Sugar Bowl
game with Alabama, the one in which we got beat so badly.
Those things don't always work out.

When we went down to Lawrence in 1967 and got beat
by Kansas, we had that guy Festus from Gunsmoke — Ken
Curtis was his name — talk to the players the morning of
the game. Boy, did that one ever backfire. Festus was staying at the same hotel as the team, so I asked him if he'd
give our players a little talk to loosen them up before we
played Kansas. Our record was 3-0, and we were feeling
pretty good about things. I don't think we figured Kansas
could beat us. So anyway, Festus climbed on the bus before
we left for the stadium and gave the players a pep talk that
loosened 'em up all right. I don't remember what he said. I

think he just kidded with them a little bit. We were looser than hell and we got beat 10-0. I can only remember being shut out four times as a college football coach, and that was one of them. Our first year at Wyoming, we tied Brigham Young, 0-0, and that Kansas game was the first time we had been shut out since I came to Nebraska. In 1968 we were shut out twice, by Oklahoma, 47-0, and by Kansas State, 12-0 in Lincoln.

There's one I'd like to forget, the Kansas State game in 1968. It was our Homecoming game, and we had less than 200 yards of offense. I think the most pressure I ever put on a team, the hardest I ever drove players in all my life, was the week after we lost to Kansas State here in Lincoln. We were going to play out in Colorado the next week, and all of the coaches got on the players real bad. We were nasty because we knew the only chance we had at Colorado was to get the players aroused. We beat CU, 22-6. Joe Orduna scored a couple of touchdowns, and Guy Ingles returned a punt 62 yards for a touchdown.

I remember Ingles told me one time: "When I'm back there receiving punts, all I do is, I stand there thinking, 'Oh God, please don't let me drop the ball because I don't want to run off the field and face Coach Devaney.'" Guy could catch a football. I don't know that he ever dropped a punt. I've always felt that the most important thing a punt returner ever had to do was catch the ball; you just can't have people fumbling the ball on punts. One year we were in such bad shape for a punt returner that we had a fullback by the name of Al Larsen, from Sioux City, back on punts. Al couldn't run very fast; he had just average speed. But Al sure could catch a football.

Getting back to motivating players before a game, I remember while I was at Wyoming, we had a magician perform prior to a game with Kansas. We had him do some tricks to relax the guys because we were about to play a team that they thought was going to kill them. I've mentioned that Kansas team before. It had John Hadl, Curtis McClinton and some other fine players. At that time, we were a fairly average football team by comparison. We thought we'd damn well better get our kids relaxed, and it turned out they played a pretty good ball game. We tied Kansas, 6-6. There might have been some magic involved in that.

Then there was the time we were going out to play Colorado in 1966. One night at practice the week before, I found one of those old-time football helmets and gave it to Don Bryant. I said: "Don, put this helmet on and come out to practice. Tell the players you just found Mike Corgan's old helmet." So right at the end of practice, I got the whole team together on the field and told them that "Coach" Bryant had a little announcement to make. Out he came in that old leather helmet, with no face mask, of course, and he said: "Notre Dame was going through their archives the other day, and they came across Coach Corgan's old helmet and sent it to us." Mike was a good halfback at Notre Dame, and he also played one year with the Detroit Lions in the National Football League. He saw Don Bryant with that helmet on, and he said: "You fat little SOB." The players loved it.

That was on a Thursday, which was the day we always let up a little in practice. We'd work the players real hard Monday through Wednesday and then ease off. Thursday was also the day some of the coaches used to gather at the Elks Club. We had a little group of local business people who would meet there in the evening with us.

We were out in Boulder playing Colorado in 1966, and we were down 19-7 at halftime to a team that really wasn't very good. We got on our players real bad at the half, as bad as I can ever remember. The Colorado players might even have heard it all because both teams were in the same barn of a fieldhouse. That's the game that Eddie Crowder came out on the field to check the clock. It had been stopped when he didn't think it should have been, and he came right out to his team's huddle to talk to one of the officials. Then, toward the end of the game, Eddie wanted just the opposite. He wanted it stopped when they were

You'd think I was born with a clipboard in my hands. Everytime
I picked one up, someone snapped a picture.

running the clock. We were still down 19-7 heading into the fourth quarter, when we scored two touchdowns to win the game. Pete Tatman made the winning touchdown with less than a minute to play, and Eddie claimed that the guy running the clock had done something wrong and shouldn't have shut off the clock, or should have and didn't — I don't remember exactly which it was. Anyway, he was bitching about it, and I said: "Heck Eddie, the timekeeper is one of your own guys." I'll never forget Eddie standing out there on the field, waving his arms like a wild man.

Bob Churchich had a great game passing that day. We went into the spread formation and he started hitting the two ends, Tom Penney and Denny Morrison, with a bunch of out patterns and short hooks. Churchich set some passing records in that game, and we were able to remain undefeated.

There's another interesting story about our next game in that 1966 season, when we beat Missouri here in Lincoln, 35-0. That was the game where Danny Devine sent Black Jack Harry Smith, one of his assistant coaches, over to the Nebraska sideline because he thought the chain gang was screwing Missouri. Black Jack Harry used to play pro football for the Detroit Lions, and he was a tough son-of-a-gun; that's why they called him "Black Jack." He was one heckuva football player, but really, he was a nice guy. I met him when I applied for the Missouri job before I went out to Wyoming from Michigan State. Harry took me around the campus at Missouri and showed me the place. I liked Harry. But Dan Devine thought he was getting a bad deal with the chains, so he sent Harry over to our sideline to keep an eye on the chain gang. Harry wasn't the type of guy you just told to leave, and when somebody came over to me and pointed Harry out, I said: "I'm certainly not going to go over and get him out of here!" Every time the chain gang came by, there was Harry following along, watching every move they made, making sure they spotted things right. I think someone did say: "Well, Harry, it's great to see you again, but you should get your butt on the other side of the field." I did ask why he was on our sideline, and he said Dan had sent him. He was embarrassed about it.

Dan Devine was coaching for Duffy at Michigan State when he got his first head coaching job at Arizona State. Bill Yeoman, another one of Duffy's assistants, was the leading candidate for the Arizona State job, but Bill had only been at Michigan State one year. Dan went into Duffy's office and said, "Here's a guy that you're letting get that Arizona State job, and he's only been with you a year while I've been with you five." Dan told Duffy that he should get the job. I'm not so sure Dan wasn't right. Bill had some connections at Arizona State, and those people had greased the skids for him, and it looked like he was all set to get the job when Duffy came to Dan's aid and got him the job instead. Bill was pretty upset. The irony of the whole thing was, later on, when Bill was at Houston and Dan was at Notre Dame, they played each other in the Cotton Bowl at the end of the 1978 season. That game had one of the most remarkable comebacks ever. Bill had Notre Dame down, 34-14, yet he got beat by Notre Dame, 35-34. Bill Yeoman was probably as upset about that loss as any in his career. I've never talked to Bill about that game, but it really had to be a disappointment when you consider all the factors, including the fact that Bill tried for a fourth-and-one late in the game and didn't make it. It wasn't that Bill disliked Danny as a person, but he didn't have a whole lot of respect for Dan's ability to coach football. Bill has done a great job of building the program at Houston and is the originator of the veer offense, while Dan Devine had a great coaching record at Arizona State, Missouri and Notre Dame.

I was talking about motivation, though. Some teams are able to rise to the occasion without the coaches doing anything special to motivate them, and some teams do unusual things that the coaches don't seem to have any control over. Missouri has always been like that. They can really get up for a big game with Southern California or some team like that one week and then fall on their face the next. I remember in 1972, we beat Missouri 62-0 here and then the next Saturday, they went up to South Bend and beat Notre Dame, 30-26. That was kind of their way of life, so to speak, as far as football was concerned. They'd beat teams that they were expected to lose to, like the Southern Cal's, the Notre Dame's and the Alabama's, and then they'd turn around and lose some games they should have won. A couple of years ago, one of Al Onofrio's teams beat USC in their opener and then lost real bad to a not-very-good Illinois team the next weekend in Columbia. Missouri has always been able to rise to the occasion, which indicates that they've got some good people playing for them, but they've never been a very consistent football team. I don't know what causes that; coaches can get a team keyed up sometimes, but they can only get a team to an emotional peak a very few times in a season. That "win one for your grandmothers, your aunts and uncles, the guys who got killed in a plane crash" stuff isn't going to work very often.

I'll tell you a little story about that, one that I like to use at banquets now and then. Before a big game, the coach told his players: "Now, we've asked you to go out and win for your father, your mother, your sisters, your brothers, and all of that . . . why not go out there this time and just win one for yourselves." Well, those players came in at the halftime, and they were just getting the hell beat out of them, so the coach said: "Okay; it's very evident you don't want to win one for yourselves, so how about thinking about the eight assistant coaches, their 27 children, and the head coach and his family."

We tried to handle each game differently. If we were the underdog, we'd try to get the kids believing that they could win. Before other games, we tried to be fairly matter-of-fact in our approach. When we were about to play Oklahoma, for example, the guys always knew we were playing for the Big Eight championship, and we figured, if they couldn't get themselves up for a game like that, they were never going to get up for anything. Where we made our worst mistakes were games in which we took teams too lightly or thought they were better than they actually were. I know we made a very glaring mistake, or at least I did, when we played Colorado in 1967. Colorado looked very powerful that year, and it looked to me like we had to gamble if we were going to win. I thought we'd have to go all out and throw all caution to the wind just trying to win the ball game. Well, it turned out that Colorado wasn't nearly as good as I thought they were, and if we'd have played them a down-to-earth, everyday football game, we would have beaten them. As it was, they scored two touchdowns on real long pass interception returns, and we lost, 21-16. We beat them in every category except points.

To digress again for a moment, the whammy Nebraska has on Colorado is one of the mysteries of sports, how one team can dominate another, year-in and year-out, no matter how good the teams are in relation to each other. It's like that for us in some ways against Oklahoma. When Colorado plays Nebraska, they seldom play their best football, and when we play Oklahoma, we don't always seem to play our best. I don't think we go into the Oklahoma game thinking we're going to lose; that's not it at all. But I think we often seem tight when we go into an Oklahoma game, and I think the same thing applies — even more so — when Colorado gets ready to play us. There's a little of Murphy's Law involved in it. You subconsciously expect things to go wrong and they do.

When I coached at Nebraska, we had some close games with Oklahoma State, but we never lost to them. We never did get beat by Iowa State, either. We got beat by Kansas twice, once each by Colorado and Kansas State, and by Missouri four times. We lost to them in 1962, and then three years in a row, 1967, 1968 and 1969. We won the other seven. The Missouri rivalry was always a very intense rivalry partly because Dan Devine and I both coached as assistants at Michigan State at the same time. While there was no personal animosity between the two of us, we both wanted to win very badly, and Missouri, of course, always had what we felt was a good group of football players to pick from. Also, I had applied for that job at Missouri. Frank Broyles got the job when I was told that I was the top candidate. Anyway, I ended up here and Danny eventually ended up down there. I would always just as soon beat Missouri as anybody, including Oklahoma.

Oklahoma was the only Big Eight team I didn't have a winning record against in my 11 seasons at Nebraska. We won five times and lost six, some of which I thought we should probably have won.

In a lot of years we figured if we could beat Missouri and Oklahoma, we would win the Big Eight championship. I think we had better balance in the Big Eight back then than we've had for awhile. Today, it comes down pretty much to Oklahoma and Nebraska, and occasionally Missouri. Missouri slipped in there to tie us for the championship in 1969, and they went to the Orange Bowl. A year or two before we got here, Missouri won a championship because Kansas had to forfeit a game. So anyway, we always felt Missouri came close to the title, but they never really quite made it over the hill. I don't know why. When we were coaching here, Colorado sometimes could come up with a good football team. Kansas used to have some good teams, now and then, and even Kansas State, when they had Lynn Dickey, Mack Herron and that bunch. Iowa State had some reasonably good individuals, too. There weren't many years when most of the Big Eight teams didn't have something. At that time, as far as the overall strength of teams was concerned, the Big Eight Conference was rightfully regarded as the top conference in the country.

As for the Big Ten, the area I came from, we never lost to a Big Ten Conference team while I was at Nebraska. We didn't play too many, but we beat Minnesota eight times and they had some good teams then. The other Big Ten teams I can remember playing while I was here were Michigan and Wisconsin. We only played Michigan the one time,

My 100th collegiate coaching victory came against Iowa State in 1969.

in my first season here, but we won in Ann Arbor, 25-13, and as I've said many times, that was one of the most important victories we had in the early years I was at Nebraska. An interesting note, in 11 seasons, we only lost two season-opening games. In 1969, we lost to Southern Cal 31-21, and then in my last year, 1972, we lost to UCLA, 20-17.

Well, getting back to what I was talking about, I overestimated Colorado in 1967. In 1968, I made another mistake, only that time I underestimated Kansas State. I could not get myself to think that we were going to get beaten by Kansas State, and as a result, we weren't mentally up for that game; it was embarrassing because it was the only time we lost to Kansas State while I was at Nebraska. So anyway, those were two games where we were just completely wrong. The rest of the time, or at least most of it, I don't think we lost a ball game because we had improperly prepared ourselves mentally for an opponent. I don't think that perhaps we worked quite hard enough for the UCLA game in 1972. I know we weren't as well-prepared for UCLA as we should have been, and it was probably the same when we played to a 23-23 tie with Iowa State that year over in Ames. I don't think we went into that game as well-prepared as we should have been, either. But neither of those times did we totally underestimate our opponents the way we did with Kansas State in 1968.

I had one guy who roamed the sidelines at home games for 25 years tell me kids automatically wanted to play football for me because when they made mistakes, I had the ability to sense when to chew them out and when to stay with them. I don't know if that's true, but I know there's a delicate line you have to walk in that area. If a kid makes a mistake because he's loafing or not trying, I think a coach has the right to jump all over him. But if the kid gets physically beaten, there's nothing you can do about it. For instance, if some guy beats him on a pass, and the guy is a little faster than he is, or, if he tries hard to make a tackle and bounces off some big bruising fullback, that's one thing. There isn't much you can say. If a kid makes a mental error, however, then I think you've got to talk to him about what he did wrong in order to make certain that he knows where he made his mistake. You know that players always feel bad when they make mistakes, but certain mistakes are different than others. The way you approach a player about it depends on the type of mistake he's made.

There have been times when I chewed a player out and then felt bad about it later. Maybe one of the coaches up in the press box would say someone missed his block real badly, and the kid would come off the field and say it wasn't him while I was chewing him out. Then we'd take a look at the films on Sunday and find out that the kid was right, that it wasn't his fault. That's the difficult part, and that's one reason we started grading films at Nebraska. At first, we'd just watch the films in a casual manner and we'd see a couple of good plays a guy would make. We'd think, "Geez, this guy played one heck of a good football game." At the same time, we'd get down on some other guy who wasn't doing these noticeable things. When we checked the films a little closer and actually started grading them, sometimes the guy we thought had played a good game, played a very poor game overall, and the guy who we had been critical of may have played a darn good football game. I think that's one reason I finally got it through my head that there's no sense of being real nasty to a kid when he comes off the field. There's always a chance you might be wrong.

I tell you, though, the only time I ever even touched a player happened when we were down in El Paso for a Sun Bowl game and I found one of our players drunk and sound asleep in his motel room. He couldn't even wake up to talk to me, he was so drunk, and I kicked him right in the butt. He knew he deserved it.

You know, Frank Kush had all that trouble about slapping a player when he was at Arizona State. Chuck Fairbanks went down there and testified at the trial, and everybody jumped all over him because he said something like coaches kicked players and grabbed their face masks because football teams are "families." One of the big newspapers covering the trial didn't think that was the way a family should be treated. They said that's "child abuse." Well, there are coaches who will do that sort of thing, but then, heck, there are coaches who'll try to get out there and demonstrate how to block and tackle and all that stuff, which can get a little foolish, too. I used to do some of that when I was coaching in high school, but I was a lot younger then. I've known of high school coaches who got out and scrimmaged with their players, but it's something I don't recommend, especially at the college level. I firmly believe that each individual coach has his own way of correcting mistakes and disciplining players. But, by the time I got to coaching in college, I wasn't going to demonstrate anything to a college player, and I wasn't about to reach up and slap one of them in the face.

chapter eighteen

*Our first national championship
and some of the people
who got us there*

Some people called our first national championship in 1970 the one-day season because so much happened in the bowl games that New Year's Day. Joe Theismann helped Notre Dame upset No. 1 Texas in the Cotton Bowl. Ohio State was No. 2 and had the chance to move up, but Jim Plunkett passed them silly and Stanford took Woody Hayes out in the Rose Bowl. We'd been rooting for the triple miracle since the bowl matchups were announced, and all that was left for us to do was beat LSU in the Orange Bowl.

So much had happened in six hours, it was almost unbelievable. We'd been tied early in the season at Southern Cal, but it was all there, right in front of us. All we had to do was go out and beat LSU. We weren't a great football team that night, but at least we got the job done and that's something Texas and Ohio State couldn't say on that particular day.

We had the same kind of opportunity in 1965 and didn't come through. We were also unbeaten and ranked No. 3 going into the bowl games that year. Duffy had Michigan State rated No. 1, but they were upset by UCLA in the Rose Bowl. Arkansas was No. 2, and LSU upset them in the Cotton Bowl. We were No. 3, and Alabama beat us in the Orange Bowl, 39-28. Steve Sloan was not a great passer, but we made him look like the best in the country in that game. He completed 20 of 28 for 296 yards and two touchdowns.

Sloan had a great receiver in Ray Perkins, who was one of the best players we ever had to play against at Nebraska. Alabama had a great linebacker, too, in LeRoy Jordan. He may have been the best we had to play against.

A lot of players pop into my mind as being among the best we faced. In the Big Eight, there was Jack Mildren and Steve Owens of Oklahoma. Gale Sayers of Kansas had a 99-yard touchdown against us. I'm not so sure Walt Garrison of Oklahoma State wasn't the toughest of all for us to tackle. When we went unbeaten in 1965, we almost got beat in Stillwater, 21-17. I remember how that game ended. On the last play, Garrison ripped off an 18-yard run and Billy Johnson tackled him at our five-yard line. After the game, I went over to congratulate Garrison, just like I'd done after George Mira almost beat us in the Gotham Bowl. Those players were all great. So were a couple of players from Minnesota, Carl Eller and Bobby Bell. They fit in the same category.

Fortunately, when everything was on the line against LSU in the Orange Bowl, we didn't have to play a great offensive team like Alabama had been five years before. LSU had a great defensive team. To be honest, though, we thought we should beat LSU, and we were all a little surprised when they played us so close.

When we went up, 10-0, a lot of people thought the score might get worse. Maybe we were too high. We'd watched Texas get beat on TV, and we'd heard the Ohio State score right before we went out for the kickoff. For some reason,

Jerry Tagge's touchdown against LSU was the most historic in Nebraska history. It gave us our first national championship.

we let down a little. LSU came back and went ahead of us, 12-10, on the last play of the third quarter. We came back like champions. When we had to have it, we did. Jerry Tagge drove us 67 yards for the winning touchdown. He did a beautiful job. He hit passes to Dan Schneiss and John Rodgers, then completed a 17-yard pass to Jeff Kinney to put the ball on the LSU five-yard line. With six minutes left, Tagge leaped into the end zone. Just about every Nebraska football fan has seen a picture of that touchdown. Tagge leaned forward, stretched out the ball with his hands and held it up in a big pile of people. That picture still hangs over my desk because of what it meant to our program.

I could tell when Tagge and Kinney were sophomores that they were part of a special group. They came back from a loss at Missouri and won their last seven games. They beat the hell out of Georgia in the Sun Bowl, 45-6. That set the tone for the back-to-back national championships. We had exceptional talent. The pro draft proved it. Nebraska hadn't had a first-round draft pick since Bob Brown in 1963. Then, in 1972, we had three. Tagge went to the Green Bay Packers. Kinney went to the Kansas City Chiefs, and Jacobson went to the New York Giants. Tagge and Kinney got most of the headlines from that team, and Rodgers and Glover got most of the headlines the next year. People have a tendency to overlook Jacobson, even though he won the Outland Trophy after our first national championship.

Big Jake was a great athlete. He was a good basketball player. When he was a sophomore in high school, he was already 6-5 and could long jump over 21 feet. When he grew to be fairly big, he used his leverage and his quickness more than his strength. Jacobson was important to us right away. The spring after his freshman year, he wore a Black Shirt because Dave Walline had mononucleosis. He played behind Walline as a sophomore and got quite a bit of playing time. Walline was a very quiet kid from Michigan. He's a dentist now and has been fighting a courageous battle

Jerry Tagge and Willie Harper, the MVP's in the 1971 Orange Bowl, smile despite the snow after our arrival back in Lincoln.

with a deteriorating disease. I've always had a lot of respect for him. Jacobson commanded respect, too. He might
have been a great pro player. He started every game for the
Giants as a rookie, then he missed the next season with a
severed tendon. When he broke a leg and missed another
season, he decided to retire. He's done well for himself as a
stockbroker.

Although Willie Harper never won the Outland Trophy,
I'd have to put him in the same class with Jacobson and
Glover. Bill Thornton recruited Willie out of Toledo, Ohio.
I knew the first minute he stepped on the field that he had
All-American possibilities. All we had to decide was where
he should play. We made him a middle guard his freshman
year. Then Mike Wynn and Sherwin Jarmon graduated
from that 1969 Sun Bowl team, so we had to find a defensive end the following spring. Willie was a natural. We
knew he was too great an athlete to redshirt. We never
thought twice about making the switch. He had a great
sophomore season, and ended it by being named the Defensive Player of the Game in the Orange Bowl. He was an All-
American as a junior and again as a senior, and he played
like one as a sophomore. They talk a lot about Hugh Green
of Pitt. Harper is in the same class. He didn't get that
many tackles when he was a senior because no one dared
run his way. He and John Dutton were on the same side,
and Glover was cleaning everything up in the middle.
When you consider all the sacks and the tackles for losses
those three had, I bet our opponents didn't gain a hundred
yards on that side of the ball the whole season. Harper had
tremendous quickness. He was almost impossible to knock
off his feet and he was perfect for the defensive scheme we
played. He's still starting in the NFL, as a linebacker for
the San Francisco 49ers. He's also a successful businessman. I'm not surprised by either. Willie was one of the
all-time greats at Nebraska.

Glover also was a great college football player, but he
was going nowhere with all the defensive tackles we had.
Monte Kiffin had Jacobson, Dutton, Monte Johnson and

President Nixon came to Lincoln to present Nebraska's
first national championship trophy.

Bill Janssen. He didn't know what to do. Johnson and Dutton weren't even good enough to start. Rich started the first game his sophomore year, but Jacobson came on strong, so Glover spent the rest of the year coming into games when they were over or somebody was hurt. We wondered what we were going to do with him. Finally, I told Monte that if Glover wasn't good enough to play tackle, we better move him to middle guard. Monte wondered if he was quick enough to play there. We found out the first day. Doug Dumler was a great center for us and he had a helluva time trying to handle Glover in practice — although he could handle anybody else in a game. We knew then and there that it was a great move for us and a great move for Glover. In my opinion, he was the best middle guard in college football during the 1970s.

Speaking of great middle guards, we had another one earlier — Wayne Meylan — who was as valuable to us in the '60s as Glover was in the '70s. Meylan was an all-American for two years.

Considering Glover's background, it's amazing how soft-spoken and kind-hearted Rich was and still is. He grew up in a tough neighborhood and went to a tough high school in Jersey City, N.J. There were 10 children in his family. Actually, we were lucky to recruit Richie. Monte went to his high school to recruit Daryl White. The powers weren't recruiting Glover. The only people interested were schools like New Mexico, Wyoming and Villanova. When it got down to offering scholarships, those schools didn't even offer Glover. Monte was the only one who did. I know it's hard to believe, but Glover might not have played college football if we hadn't decided to recruit him. We wouldn't have given him a scholarship if we didn't think he had a chance. But we never dreamed he would be the great player he was. It's a tribute to him and a tribute to Monte, who had a special way to motivate his players. Glover set goals for himself, then worked his butt off to meet them. He's one of the most dedicated players we ever had. If he missed a practice or a meeting, no one can remember it. He was a

Little Eddie Periard and big Larry Jacobson each grab a leg and carry me off the field after we beat Oklahoma, 28-21, in 1970.

great team player. We built our defense around him and a
lot of times, that would tie him down, so others could look
good. If it was for the good of the team, he took on the assignment. He never complained. He never let anything
written or said about him affect his play. Rich was so
steady and so consistent, we almost took him for granted.
Another great thing about Rich Glover — you could always count on him being at his best when you needed him
most. His best performances were in the biggest games.

Kinney and Rodgers got a lot of the attention from the
Game of the Century against Oklahoma, but if we hadn't
had Glover, we never would have stopped Oklahoma that
day. He was just as important to that victory as they were.
He just smashed Oklahoma's inside game. OU had an All-
American center, Tom Brahaney. Glover was determined
not to let him explode off the ball. He played him so close,
it looked like their helmets were welded together when
they lined up. Glover finished with 22 tackles that day.
The television cameras couldn't keep from zeroing in on
him almost every play. Since that game had the largest TV
audience in the history of college football, Glover became
somewhat of a celebrity. I'm still convinced that performance set the stage for him to win the Outland and Lombardi Trophies the following season. Some centers never really knew how strong Rich Glover was because they never
touched him. He just dominated people, even when they
double-teammed him. I can honestly say Glover never
played a bad football game for us. He was always somewhere between outstanding and super.

I've had fans come up to me and ask why I pushed John
Rodgers for the Heisman Trophy and not Rich Glover. The
truth is, I said if I was forced to vote and had to pick one,
I'd flip a coin. Deep down, that's the way I felt. That was-
n't going to help either one, so I decided it was more realistic to promote Rodgers because there had never been an in-
terior lineman win the Heisman in the history of college
football. Glover would have been a good exception and he
would have deserved the honor. However, if I would have

pushed him, he would have been a longshot to win it and it would have hurt Rodgers' chances at the same time.

Glover got a lot of publicity anyway. When he followed Jacobson with the Outland Trophy, it was the first time the same school had won the award back-to-back. The media made a big deal out of that. Glover also beat some great linemen out for the Lombardi Trophy that year. Oklahoma's center, Brahaney, was a finalist. So was Jerry Sisemore, a tackle from Texas and John Hannah, the guard from Alabama. Winning the Lombardi is a major accomplishment. Rich was flown to Houston and sat next to Ronald Reagan and his wife at the banquet. He got to meet Frank Leahy, the great Notre Dame coach, and Marie Lombardi, Vince's widow. His trophy was a 45-pound block of granite mounted on a silver pedestal. It wasn't the Heisman, but it meant just as much.

Pro scouts saw Glover's future the same as they see most college middle guards. Like Jim Stillwagon of Ohio State and Granville Liggins of Oklahoma, they thought he was better suited for pro football in Canada. Rich was 6-1 and 234 pounds. He was really too short for the NFL and wasn't really fast enough to be a linebacker. That's why the Giants drafted Rich in the third round. Even though his teammates voted him their Rookie of the Year, he only lasted one more season with the Giants. Then he spent a year in the World Football League. Then, just when everyone thought it was all over for Rich, he came back and started every game for the Philadelphia Eagles. When the Eagles hired Dick Vermeil, Rich got cut. He spent three years as a defensive line coach at Washington State. Now he's an estate planner in San Jose and the defensive coordinator at San Jose City College. We still keep in touch on the phone. No. 79 was one of the greatest at Nebraska. That's why we retired his jersey.

chapter nineteen

The Johnny Rodgers case caused more soul-searching than anything I've ever done

I may be wrong, but I'm betting that people are more interested in what I have to say about Johnny Rodgers than anything else I mention in the book. It's only natural. John was the best player I ever coached. He's the only Heisman Trophy winner we've ever had. And he's probably the most controversial athlete you'll ever see around here.

I know people are curious to hear my views on the gas station robbery and all that stuff. But I feel more comfortable starting The Johnny Rodgers Story where it begins — when we first started recruiting him out of Omaha Tech. We knew even then that John was a great talent. You could tell on film that he had a tremendous ability to run with the football and a tremendous ability to catch it. He was more of a running back in high school.

We never took John for granted. We knew some of the powers would try to go into Omaha for a player like him. When we heard how interested USC was, we decided to recruit John as hard as you recruit anybody.

John Rodgers did a lot of sweating   before he won the Heisman.

John's real father lived in California, so that was a concern. We felt we needed some extra help in Omaha, so we talked to Everett Alger. He was very influential in helping us recruit John. He stayed in touch with Rodgers and lined up a summer job for him.

When he finally signed his letter of intent, we were happier than we'd ever been about an in-state recruit. The Shrine Bowl game that summer just reinforced what we already knew — John could catch better than anyone and run with just about anyone. Even though he was an I-back as a freshman, we envisioned him as a great wingback.

Obviously, we weren't wrong. John was probably the best wingback college football has ever seen and it may be a long time before we see another one like him.

Anyone who watched John Rodgers play football, basketball or baseball in high school knew what kind of an athlete he was. When he got to Nebraska, he was an immediate star with the freshman team. More than anything, he showed what he could do one-on-one. He led the freshman team in rushing, scoring and kick returns. He was great in the broken field. We had a pretty good slotback in Jeff Hughes, but we knew Rodgers had more talent. He would have been the last guy in the world to redshirt.

John's sophomore season on our first national championship team was even more than we expected. He was the best sophomore in the Big Eight and probably the best sophomore in the country. He scored in every game but one. He caught more than 700 yards in passes and rushed for more than 200 yards. He had nothing but greatness staring him in the face. I couldn't think of anything that would hold him back.

Then it happened. I was attending a Big Eight meeting that next spring in Stillwater. Don Bryant and I got called out of the meeting for a telephone call. His secretary was on one line and my secretary was on the other. We both hung up the phone and just looked at each other. The news was out. John had robbed a gas station as a last-day-of-school prank his freshman year. The police had caught some kid doing something and he told them that if they thought that was bad, he'd robbed a gas station the year before with Johnny Rodgers. By that time, everybody had heard of Johnny Rodgers. The police called him in and he confessed right away. He didn't know why he'd done it, but he did. He said he'd thought about giving the $90 back to the gas station, but didn't know how to go about it.

God, we were talking about armed robbery. I remember all of us thinking it was all over — there was no way he was going to play football again. I pictured him behind bars, not in the end zone. I remember how sorry I felt for him. Life hadn't been easy for John and now it was worse.

Agonizing over the whole Johnny Rodgers' situation was the hardest thing I've ever done. I stayed awake nights trying to decide what to do. I knew there was no right answer. If we kept him on the team, people would think we'd do anything just to win. If we kicked him off, we'd be kicking his life away. Most poeple would think justice had prevailed. But what would it do to the only person that really mattered. What would it do to John Rodgers? Every coaching meeting we had, we discussed John. We didn't know how we were going to allow him back on the team.

The trouble was, we were convicting him before the courts were. The public sentiment was definitely against letting him back on the team, but our main concern was trying to do what was right, not what was popular. I think Tom Osborne was the first guy to bring it up. He said if the courts decide to put John on probation, why shouldn't we do the same thing? Yes, John was a football player, but the crime did not occur during football season and it sounded a hell of a lot worse than it was.

We were concerned about due process, so we called the university attorneys in to discuss the situation with them. John had played a whole season after the robbery. He hadn't been in trouble before or since. If the courts were going to treat him as a first-time offender, we felt we had to do the same thing.

The kid who told the police about John was white. If he

Johnny Rodgers and the Heisman Trophy.

got off on probation, would we be unduly penalizing John by doing something more punitive and taking away his scholarship? Based on his record, our attorneys felt John might be able to sue the school, if we kicked him off and jeopardized his career. We didn't discuss this with the press, but it was an angle we hadn't thought about. It made the decision even tougher. Nebraska is a very conservative state. Rodgers had been involved in a major crime. He was a kid from the big, bad inner-city of Omaha. Not very many people were on his side.

You could have had the biggest political race, the biggest tax issue or the biggest No. 1 argument in the history of Nebraska. But I don't know if any would have created more conversation in the coffee shops and the bars than John Rodgers did. Everyone in the state had an opinion. Everyone knew he'd done something very wrong. He'd disappointed thousands of young people who idolized him. For them, John probably deserved to be suspended.

But an old phrase kept popping into my mind — two wrongs don't make a right. The University Student Tribunal said it was okay for John to continue school. The court said he was free to pursue normal activities. His crime was against society and he was given the go-ahead in society by the court. His crime was not against the football team and did not affect either his performance or the performance of his teammates.

The court treated John as a citizen, not as a football star. I couldn't help remembering the Johnny Roland case at Missouri. He'd gotten caught stealing some tires, so Missouri suspended him from school for a year. Then they changed their mind and suspended him only one semester, so he played football that next spring. Roland got a second chance and made the most of it. He turned his life around and became a very successful pro with the St. Louis Cardinals.

But John's case was different. The university was not suspending him. Maybe I got to rationalizing, I don't know. This all happened at a time when individual rights were really becoming important. I didn't know if I was mellowing or what. All I knew was my record wasn't perfect. If people hadn't given me a second chance, there was no telling where I'd have been. I thought that if we took football away from John, he might not want to stay in school and if he didn't stay in school, he really wouldn't have a chance. The threat of a lawsuit didn't end up entering into my decision at all. It was just something that was brought up. Finally, I just decided that if everyone else was willing to give John an opportunity to redeem himself, I was willing to do the same thing. I felt that if I deprived him a chance to play football, I'd be working against the aims of probation already established.

In my mind, John had suffered much more than anyone else under similar circumstances. I realized when you're as well-known as he had become, you lose your right to privacy. When a public figure screws up, the publicity is overwhelming. The way I look at it, that publicity is almost a greater penalty than the law can hand down. After I got back from the Coaches All-America Game in Lubbock that July, I analyzed everything again. I also decided to put John on two years probation. I put the ball in his hands. It was up to him to run with it or fumble it. I've never in my life spent so much time on one thing. But I'm glad I did. I have no regrets. Keeping John on the football team was the right thing to do.

That doesn't mean it was all peaches and cream for John the rest of the time he was at the university. But he kept himself in line and I give Tom Osborne almost all the credit for that.

Tom was the receivers coach and John was the type who was a little irresponsible about attending a meeting or being where he was supposed to be at the right time. John didn't skip practice, but when he was late, Tom would tell him to meet him at the track at 6 o'clock the next morning. John hated two things: he hated running and he hated to get up in the morning. But if he didn't, Tom just doubled the penalty. So John would be out there and Tom would run with him. One thing about Tom — he kept John on the straight and narrow path while he was playing for us. Tom developed him into a great football player and kept him in tow at the same time.

I hate to sound like a lawyer giving a closing statement 11 years after the fact. I feel like I'm talking in circles. But I'm trying to explain everything that went through my mind during that whole deal with Johnny Rodgers. Through the years, I've run into enough people to know that not everyone buys my logic. They think the only reason I gave John a break was because he was a great player. A lot more went into it than that. But I'm not going to deny that as a coach, it wasn't a pleasant thought to picture a football team without John when you've already seen what he can do. I don't care what anybody says, every coach in the United States would like to keep his best player on the team. Even the straightest coaches will roll with the punches, if they think they can help an athlete turn his life around and keep them in the winning column.

Look at Bear Bryant. Joe Namath gave him fits. Finally, he kicked him off the team one year. Then Joe lived right in the basement of his house. Bear did not give up on Joe. If he would have given up, that would have been it. Joe might not have ever turned things around for himself. Everybody wants to win. Sometimes, it may look like you are bending the rules to accommodate the stars, but it's just a different world. Kids grow up under a lot more pressure these days. There's also a lot more temptation out there. Things don't go easy for everyone. John Rodgers grew up with his brother and sister in a two-room house while his mother barely made ends meet on a welfare check. People can criticize John Rodgers all they want. They can call him a criminal. They can make him their favorite racist joke. But I'd like to see how damn good they'd turn out, growing up in poverty without a father. I wouldn't wish that kind of life on anyone. John still pays publicly for the one big mistake he made. Considering where he came from and the way he had to come up, it's amazing he didn't make a lot more mistakes.

Public sentiment was against Rodgers then and for all I know, it may still be against him now. We got a lot of letters criticizing us for playing John. Fortunately, his success as an individual and our success as a team helped reduce that criticism. I'm sure if we'd played John and gotten beat, we'd have heard a lot more criticism than we did. The only good thing about the whole situation was the timing. At least it cropped up after we'd already won our first national championship. People knew John was an important part of that team, but we had a lot of offensive players people talked about — Joe Orduna, Jeff Kinney, Jerry Tagge, Van Brownson, Dan Schneiss, Guy Ingles. Bob Newton was an All-American lineman. John was a sensational sophomore that year, but so was Doug Dumler, our center. And so was Willie Harper, one of our defensive ends. Contrary to the way people remember it, John was not the whole show and I'm glad he wasn't. It took some pressure off.

That second national championship team was loaded and Rodgers probably won as many All-American honors as anyone we had. I remember him catching three touchdown passes against Minnesota that year. He had a 92-yard punt return against Oklahoma State and a 62-yard punt return against Iowa State, so that 72-yard punt return everyone talks about against Oklahoma was no fluke.

Of all the plays I've ever seen in college football, I'd have to rate that punt return in the Oklahoma game as the best. Like Bobby Reynolds' touchdown run against Missouri, John's punt return has gotten bigger and bigger over the years. I've seen it so many times on film, I've got it memorized. He slipped once, lost his balance, twisted and did just about everything else on that run. The return was set up to the right, but John saw a hole to the left and cut back. The only guy he could remember seeing was Joe Blahak. There was a strong wind blowing that day and Joe Wylie punted the ball real high and real deep. Oklahoma's coverage got downfield so fast, I thought John should have called for a fair catch. I'm sure it didn't even enter his mind. He caught the ball with Greg Pruitt breathing down his neck. He took the hit and spun around to keep from falling. If Pruitt hadn't hit him on one side, another Oklahoma player was in position to hit him on the other side. John took off for the right, then darted back left through a whole bunch of Oklahoma players. That's when he was open and away from the flow of the coverage. He headed for the left sideline. Blahak screened off Wylie, the last guy with a chance to tackle John. Wylie is fast, but he didn't have a very good angle on Rodgers. Johnny was starting to tire. But when Blahak took Wylie out, John could have crawled the rest of the way and still scored. That touchdown was the most important one of the game because it gave us an 11-point lead. It forced Oklahoma to battle uphill all afternoon long.

No question about it, John gave us that extra dimension. Even though he was double-teamed all year, he had almost 1,000 yards receiving his junior season. That was an unbelievable statistic, considering the coverage he got. It made the other teams vulnerable, so we could also throw the ball to people like Woody Cox and Jerry List and even Jeff Kinney. John had established himself as a superstar, but he was also a team player. He really blended in with all that talent. He had no qualms about Kinney and Tagge getting more attention than he did.

In my mind, Rodgers was the greatest punt return man I've ever seen in college football. You could put together a whole highlight film just on his punt returns. Every time he touched the ball, he was a threat to go all the way. If he got loose from the first guy, you could almost bet on him faking the next two guys out of their scholarships. He made more defensive players mad on punt returns than anything. They'd talk about him all week, think about him when they lined up . . . and he'd still burn them. He was so great on punt returns, everyone always seems to ask me why we never used John on kickoff returns. Very simply, he was not that kind of runner. Kickoff return men put their heads right straight up into that pocket and then make a break. That wasn't Rodgers' style and we weren't going to change it. We also weren't crazy about watching him get hurt on a kickoff return.

Even I'd get excited when John would stand back there, ready to field a punt. You could sense the anticipation in the stadium and on the bench. You just knew something was going to happen. Even with everyone gunning for him, John had almost 800 yards in punt returns his junior season. He was truly amazing. Part of the reason he was so great was his courage. He'd do everything in his power to avoid getting hit, but he wasn't afraid to take a shot from anybody. He had tremendous durability. He was like a shock absorber out there.

Whenever he'd get hit — no matter how hard it was — he'd bounce right back up and head for the huddle. I know there had to be times when he was biting his lip in pain. But you never heard about it. John Rodgers was as tough as they come. He was a coach's player and a player's player. He had a lot of ability and the guts to go with it.

I remember Bear Bryant talking about Rodgers before the Orange Bowl that year. He'd seen enough film to know that no matter how good your punt coverage was, you still might follow Rodgers into the end zone. Bear tried to get ready for him, but it didn't help. John was really the guy who started the rout against Alabama. We were only ahead 6-0 when Alabama punted on the last play of the first quarter. Rodgers ran it back 77 yards for a touchdown. I think that absolutely demoralized Alabama. They were madder than hell at themselves and while they worried about what had happened, we scored two more touchdowns in the second quarter. Even a coach who can walk on water has a hard time coming back from a 28-0 halftime score.

That game was a great moment for Nebraska and another great game for Johnny Rodgers. But what I saw in the locker room after the game meant more than anything I'd seen all night during the game. I saw a side of John Rodgers that I wish other people could have seen. We were unbeaten, untied and national champions again. We'd just handed Bear his first loss of the season. Everybody was in the mood to celebrate. There was a lot of whoopin' and hollerin'. The reporters were all huddling around John, sensing he was going to get the MVP award. All of a sudden, he jumped up on the bench, holding the game ball high above his head.

John yelled something like: "Hey, guys, give me your attention. I know we always put it to a vote to see who gets the game ball. But I say it should go by acclamation to one of the greatest guys there is, Rex Lowe."

The team went nuts. Rex was a very talented split end who had Hodgkins Disease. He was on the sidelines with us and had rolled his wheelchair into the locker room. He was sitting quietly over in a corner. John jumped off the bench and made his way through all the traffic. He said: "Hey, Rex, this is yours . . . from all the guys." Then he put the ball in Lowe's arms.

Rex was pretty emotional. "Aaaaw, Johnny, you're the greatest," he said. "You and all the guys in here are the greatest buddies a guy ever had." Then he started to cry. John put his arm around Rex and hugged him. Rex cried and said "thank you, thank you." John didn't say anything, but tears were running down his cheeks. Here was a strong black kid hugging a weak white kid. God, it was a touching scene for everyone — the kind you see in the movies. I didn't put it all together at the time. But looking back, I can see why John Rodgers felt something for Rex Lowe. Rex went through all that physical suffering and John went through all that emotional suffering.

Things always went well for John on the field, but they still weren't too great for him off the field. He had a real knack for being in the wrong place at the wrong time. Once, he was caught running a stop sign while driving with a suspended license. Once, they stopped him and a friend on the interstate to Omaha and tried to pin a marijuana charge on him. John was already paranoid. He thought the police were hassling him and he may have been right. They seemed to be wherever he was, no matter what time it was. John insists that the day they picked him up on the interstate, they pulled him out of the car, called him by name

and said they were busting him for possession of marijuana. They didn't even ask him for an ID. They searched
the trunk and didn't find anything. No charges were filed,
but the press wrote up the incident and John's reputation
as a wild kid got a little worse. There was a new cry to kick
him off the team. Everything that happened seemed to
make him a little more paranoid. He was called the bad guy
in so many different situations, some people started looking at John like he was a gangster. They thought he was
getting every break in the book.

chapter twenty

*After two national titles
we believed all the nice things
people were writing about us*

I wouldn't call what happened to John "getting the breaks". I thought he'd get a 30-day jail sentence because that's what everyone else was getting for driving with a suspended license. That summer before his senior year, John's lawyer appealed and I didn't know if that was good or bad. I didn't know how long you stretched out an appeal. I thought it was bad timing. I had visions of John starting to serve time the week before the Oklahoma game. If he had to serve it, I thought the sooner, the better. I would have been a little madder about his new problems if I hadn't been in court the same day he was. When he appeared for driving on the suspended license, I was in court on a speeding charge. They put us in the same story. That made us both look real good.

By this time, we hadn't lost for 32 straight games, so I guess most of the fans didn't worry about traffic violations. But I did. They caused John more problems and at that stage of his career, he didn't need any more. Despite all of his success, all these little things were adding up in his mind. John was starting to feel like people were against him. That situation with Rex Lowe showed how much John wanted to be wanted and how much he really did care. But I can't honestly say our football players were in love with John Rodgers. They all had personal lives. Whenever they'd go home, they'd pick up negative feedback. They didn't always like the image, but they knew a lot of it wasn't justified and they accepted John because of the kind of athlete he was. They wanted to win and they knew John would give them 100 percent to try and win.

I probably should have sensed things wouldn't be easy for John's senior year. I figured he and Greg Pruitt of Oklahoma would be the two leading candidates for the Heisman Trophy. I knew we were coming off two national championships. Recruiting had gotten a little easier. The biggest problem was psychological and we didn't deal with it very well. We started to believe all the nice things people were writing about us. I would have been superstitious, but I believed what Duffy Daugherty always said: "It sure is bad luck not to have good players." Everyone in the world was asking me about going for three straight national championships and if it was good luck to be rated No. 1. All I said was I'd rather start out No. 1 than start out No. 99 and try to work my way up. I knew we had some great players — Rodgers, Rich Glover, Willie Harper, Dave Mason, Jerry List, Bill Olds, Bill Janssen, John Dutton, Larry Jacobson, Doug Dumler, Bill Sloey, Jim Branch, Joe Blahak, Daryl White, Rich Sanger. People still can't believe that Monte Johnson, who started all those years at middle linebacker for the Oakland Raiders, was a second-team defensive tackle for us his senior year. I'm still not sure if that showed how much talent we had or if we underestimated Monte Johnson. He still played more than the two starters.

The coaches knew a third straight national championship was improbable, but not impossible. We knew there

Glover and Rodgers. The Outland, Lombardi, Heisman and Orange Bowl trophies in one year!

was some great talent in the country that year. LSU had Bert Jones at quarterback and Arkansas had Joe Ferguson. I would have felt a lot better if we were starting the season with one of those two guys. I thought Dave Humm and Terry Luck had good talent for sophomores and Steve Runty was a good junior prospect. But I was a little concerned about starting one of them right off the bat at UCLA. The only thing that made me feel better was UCLA being in the same boat. They didn't have an experienced quarterback either. They started Mark Harmon, son of the great Michigan All-American, Tommy Harmon. Mark is a big star on that TV show, Flamingo Road, now. And he was the star in that 1972 season-opener, too. He threw a long touchdown pass against us that night and ran for another one. He also got UCLA down there where Efren Herrera kicked a 30-yard field goal to beat us in the last 30 seconds.

As if losing wasn't a bad enough way to start my last year of coaching, Johnny Rodgers started his last year bitching about it. After we lost, he came up to me and said we should have named a black captain. He didn't say he should have been one, but he thought Rich Glover should have been one instead of Bill Janssen. A couple years later, Janssen popped off to the New York media that Rodgers was the greatest guy in the world when he was an unknown, but he became impossible when he became famous. Janssen said by the time Rodgers was a senior, he didn't have a friend on the team. I don't know about that. It may have been true. But I do know I didn't appreciate John blaming a loss on whether we had a black or a white captain. I gave him hell right then and there. I told John he was way, way off base. He and I had a little session in the locker room at UCLA. I think he expected a little sympathy for his thoughts and I wasn't about to give him the pleasure. I was pretty strong with John, but I don't know if it had much impact. I told him that anyone could react to winning. Losing is when you find out about yourself.

Well, that first loss in 33 games was my first real clue

that John Rodgers was not getting any easier to deal with. By this time, John had become very much impressed with his ability. I knew whatever pro coach got a hold of him was going to have a harder time dealing with John than I did. Like I said, Tom Osborne kept John in line and I knew he could do it one more time. I hate to sound so serious about this whole Rodgers' situation. John was a loose individual, so we loosened up occasionally ourselves. We used to say John's humility was a little like Muhammad Ali's. Tom tells the story that Rodgers got hurt once against Missouri. He was stretched out on the field, so Tom went out to see how he was. Tom asked him if he was okay. John said yes, he was going to be okay. But he wanted to know how the crowd was taking it.

Our problems with Rodgers really weren't that bad. There were times when he didn't practice, but they were physical problems. They weren't in his mind. John had an ulcer that caused a lot of stomach flu. He had some asthma, too. When those two things worked together on him, he was a pretty sick kid. Even on the days when Rodgers was supposed to be healthy, he was sick. Frosty Anderson told me that John would go over to the sidelines, vomit a couple times and go back on the field. Rodgers also had a lot of chest colds and bronchitis. He was rarely injured.

He did have thumb surgery during winter ball before his senior year. I'll never forget that. He called a press conference at Methodist Hospital in Omaha to clear up all the mystery about him being there. I couldn't believe it. John conducted the interview from a wheelchair. He was wearing lavender pajamas and a plaid robe. His arm was in a cast up to his elbow. He said he'd had the thumb problem since he got to Nebraska, but decided to have surgery so he could score at least 20 touchdowns his senior year. I don't mind setting individual goals, but that kind doesn't exactly go over in public. John couldn't stop the interview there either. Even though I hadn't made a decision about retiring, John told the press that there was a 50-50 chance that I

would. Then he said if I hired someone on the staff, there'd
be problems because everyone thought he deserved the job.
I chuckle a little bit when I think about it now. But that
should have given me some idea about where John was
coming from before his last year.

John was a daring sort of individual. When he went to
Chicago to have his picture taken for Playboy's All-America team that spring, he fell in love with the secretary of
Anson Mount, who picks the teams. Two days after John
got back to Lincoln, this secretary flew back to see him.
Mount let her take a vacation because she wasn't getting
any work done anyway. A few days later, she called Mount
from Lincoln, telling him she's quitting and marrying John
— as soon as possible. The next day, about 3 in the morning, she calls Mount back and wants him to referee a lovers'
quarrel. About dawn, he finally settles them down. The
next night, the same thing happened. During one fight, the
two destroyed most of the furniture in Willie Harper's
apartment. Within a week, the secretary was back in
Chicago, working and cussing out her boss for introducing
her to Rodgers.

Between his love affairs and his predictions, you would-
n't think John would have much time to work. But he
worked hard to make things happen for himself. He must
have known what he was talking about in that wheelchair
because he scored 21 touchdowns his senior year. He had
more than 1,000 yards receiving. I was a little surprised.
Ten of his touchdowns came by rushing. Rodgers was the
type of athlete that if he didn't get it one way, he'd get it
another way. He had an excellent senior season. He did everything for us, but he didn't have a good game against
Oklahoma. We already had the Orange Bowl bid before the
game and we went up 14-0 on Oklahoma midway through
the third quarter. Oklahoma came back and beat us, 17-14,
for the Big Eight championship.

We could have broken the Oklahoma game open that
year if today's rules had been in effect. A defensive back
pushed Rodgers out-of-bounds before he caught a touch-

down pass. Under the present rule, it would have been a touchdown. But in '72, it was against the rules for a receiver to catch the ball after he'd been knocked out-of-bounds. So they called the touchdown back. They should have called pass interference the way the defensive back played it. I hate to complain, though. There were so many plays they didn't call back on Rodgers. I guess that stuff has a way of balancing out. In my opinion, John's most memorable play at Nebraska was that punt return in the '71 Oklahoma game. At least, I remember that play more than any other. I'll admit it now — there was a questionable clip on the play. It was not a blatant thing that you'd consider a big break. It was the kind officials could either pick up or let go.

Obviously, if I had to pick which Oklahoma game I wanted to win more, it was the '71 game because it meant so much more. Still, the '72 game was a disappointing loss. And Rodgers didn't help matters much when he criticized our game plan afterwards. He said he didn't score because we didn't get the ball to him enough.

Sometimes, John didn't think very well. He didn't realize that that Oklahoma team had the best defense we played against in the 11 years I was head coach. We tried to get Rodgers the ball, but Oklahoma was all over him. That Oklahoma team had a tremendous front four and it wasn't easy getting a pass off against people like Lucious Selmon, Ray Hamilton and Derland Moore. John even did something he rarely did — he dropped the ball a couple times. I told him that when he looked at the films, he'd realize what happened in that game. Then I told the press that John would enhance his opportunities a great deal if he'd tell reporters he had a sore throat or something.

chapter twenty-one

*The top Heisman candidates,
Rodgers and Pruitt,
were both from the Big Eight*

By the Oklahoma game that year, the Heisman Trophy question had really heated up. In Rodgers and Pruitt, the Big Eight knew it had the two best candidates. Those two helped their own cause, too. They kept getting publicity about being such good friends. They were always calling each other on the phone. They'd talk to each other for an hour a shot before they realized neither one had that kind of money. They were buying each other T-shirts, talking about playing in the Hula Bowl in Hawaii and trying to upstage each other by backing into the end zone. Rodgers did it against Missouri. I didn't necessarily like it, but as long as he was getting the job done, I didn't come down on him. I didn't care how John got in the end zone — just as long as he got there.

The whole Heisman business was getting a little out of hand, though. The big question everyone was asking was if the award should be based on ability or character. Most of the Big Eight coaches, except Al Onofrio at Missouri, said they wouldn't judge what Rodgers did off the field. Even Chuck Fairbanks of Oklahoma said the Heisman should be based on ability. He thought Pruitt was the best back in the country and I did, too. I thought Rodgers was the best player. Pruitt was a sensational back, but he couldn't match Rodgers' statistics. Pruitt had rushed for almost 1,700 yards his junior year and finished third in the Heisman voting, so he had good credentials. His senior year wasn't quite as impressive. Oklahoma got beat that year by Colorado, but we got tied by Iowa State. If Rodgers hadn't caught a couple of touchdown passes against Iowa State, his stock might have gone down a little. Pruitt was starting to come on. In the two games before we played Oklahoma, he had almost 200 yards against Missouri and about 150 in the first half against Kansas. People were starting to brag him up a little more, so he and John got on the phone again and decided the Nebraska-Oklahoma game would probably decide the Heisman winner.

The big showdown never came off. Pruitt sprained his ankle in the first quarter and didn't play the rest of the game, and Rodgers bruised some ribs when he was slammed down on the AstroTurf trying to catch a pass. I think he only had 40 yards receiving and about five yards rushing that day. It was a tough day on him, but it was even tougher on Pruitt. I figured then that Rodgers would probably win the Heisman and Rich Glover would get a lot of support. I turned out to be right. Rodgers was first, Pruitt second and Glover third. Four quarterbacks followed that group — Bert Jones of LSU, Terry Davis of Alabama, John Hufnagel of Penn State and George Amundsen of Iowa State.

Because of his paranoia, I think John felt the writers on the two coasts were going to burn him in the balloting on the character issue. But they didn't. He had almost three times as many No. 1 votes as Pruitt did. Even though I lobbied pretty hard for John to win because I knew he had the best chance to win, I was glad to see Glover finish third.

He deserved it. He'd already won the Outland and Lombardi Trophies, so he won the ones most important to him. It hadn't been the kind of season I wanted, but we did stay in the national spotlight.

Rodgers' great performances took some of the sour taste out of what I considered a somewhat disappointing season. I'd rather have a national championship than a Heisman Trophy winner and I'm sure John would, too. But having a Heisman winner is the next best thing. It brings a lot of attention and adds a lot of glamour to your school. Everyone was calling Rodgers the greatest all-purpose offensive player in college football history. I couldn't come up with a better description. John did everything you can imagine with a football. In his three years as a starter, he averaged almost 14 yards every time he touched the football. He averaged 165 yards a game in all-purpose running, and he averaged one touchdown every nine times he touched the ball. In the end, I think it was John's versatility that overshadowed Pruitt, who has proven to be a better pro player than Rodgers, probably because he's been more durable.

I thought winning the Heisman would restore John's faith in people and I think it did. The vote really surprised him. There had been quite an editorial campaign about his bad-boy image and John still won in a landslide. It seemed to humble John a little bit. A lot of his flamboyance may have been a coverup. I don't know. Maybe that's why John was so flashy . . . because he was a little insecure. I tried to take that into consideration when I dealt with him. John had to pay a pretty high price for his fame. It wasn't the smoothest road to the top, but he got there. I don't see how anyone who saw Rodgers play could have voted against him. As far as I'm concerned, if the Heisman vote was supposed to say something about character, Rodgers would have won that one, too. He had the character to come back from all his troubles to play hard enough and well enough to win. Most people would have folded under the same circumstances. John Rodgers was a champion, in every sense of the word.

After he won the Heisman, I was touched when John called me a stand-in father for the real father he never knew. Unfortunately, I could not make the ceremonies on the night he received the award at the Downtown Athletic Club in New York. I had committed myself to a speaking engagement months before at the University of New Mexico. I would have felt bad about it, if Tom Osborne hadn't been able to attend the dinner. I felt it was appropriate because he'd done so much to develop Rodgers and keep him on the right path. Tom was a great motivator of people. He motivated John on and off the field. At that time, Tom was still helping counsel athletes academically. The first semester of Rodgers' junior year, John had a perfect 4.0 average. He owed a lot of things besides football to Tom.

The more John sat back and thought about his career, the more he realized how great it had been and how lucky he had been. He had experienced an awful lot in 21 years. It all started to hit home with him. He got a little emotional in his acceptance speech, especially when he mentioned Tom. He almost broke down and cried like he did when he gave Rex Lowe the game ball in the Orange Bowl. Sometimes, when John didn't feel like he had a friend in the world, Tom Osborne was there.

During Rodgers' three years, we averaged 40 points a game with Tom coordinating the offense. He had that knack to dissect a film and spot a weakness. We saw some things on film that we wanted to do against Notre Dame in the Orange Bowl. So, without telling anyone, we moved Rodgers from flanker to I-back. It proved to be quite a success. Rodgers ended his college career in a real blaze of glory. Anyone doubting if Rodgers should have won the Heisman had to change his mind after the Orange Bowl. Moving John from wingback to I-back simply meant he could handle the ball more. It wasn't done because John had complained about not getting it enough against Oklahoma. Before you wonder if that strategy would have worked against Oklahoma, consider that Notre Dame was the same team Missouri upset the week after we beat Mis-

Compliments of the Miami News after we beat
Notre Dame, 40-6, in the '73 Orange Bowl.

souri, 62-0. We were taking on a much, much weaker defensive team. Against Notre Dame, John was able to explode through the line. He carried the ball 15 times for 81 yards. That would have been a little more difficult to do against Selmon and that crew. Anyway, three of those runs were touchdowns. John also caught a 50-yard touchdown pass from Dave Humm and threw a 52-yard touchdown pass to Frosty Anderson. He put on a show the Orange Bowl had never seen before and may never see again.

John said he wanted to win the last game for me more than he wanted to win the Heisman Trophy. I think he meant it. At least he played like he did. He told writers afterwards that he was willing to run until he fell over, if that would help me win my last game. Actually, John wasn't in top shape for the game. He'd lost about 12 pounds with the flu and he only gained six of those pounds back. He wanted 100 yards rushing, but didn't get it. He admitted later that he had a new respect for running backs who gain 100 yards. It was the longest game of John's life. He proved he could run, but he also proved we had him at the right position throughout his career. He was just too small to take the kind of punishment a running back has to take. Now that people were convinced that Rodgers was one of the greatest players in college football, they started talking about the pros.

He was brilliant, but people still wondered about the pros. I was a little curious myself. I didn't know if anyone would draft him in the first round, but San Diego did. Montreal offered more money, so John was off and running. Marv Levy, Montreal's coach, probably didn't know what he was getting into. You could control John in college, but I thought it would be a different story once John got some money — something he'd never had. John left another bad mark before he graduated when his all-star basketball team didn't show up for some game in Pawnee City. All these people showed up to watch the game, but the team didn't show. John apologized later and wrote the school a check for services not rendered. He just had too many things going.

John did win Rookie of the Year honors in the Canadian League, but he still couldn't avoid controversy. He charged Montreal with racism and tried to sue the team for breach of contract. He said they attacked his reputation through the media. About this time, I was starting to wonder about John. He became a follower of some teenage guru. He wore a medallion of the guru and said he'd finally found inner peace, something that had always been missing in his life.

Things didn't go a whole lot better when John went to the San Diego Chargers. Custom agents took his Rolls Royce because he hadn't paid import duty. They said John drove his Mercedes into the country and declared it, but some friends drove his Rolls Royce through Detroit and didn't declare any duty. Somehow, John was always in the news. He had some good games with the Chargers, but he ended up filing a suit against them, too. He claimed they were negligent in the way they treated the knee injury that ended his pro career.

Finally, John let it all die a natural death. He started to make a new life for himself and was fortunate to have the money to do it. He made a few headlines during the gas shortage when he bought a service station so he and his friends wouldn't have to wait so long in line. But, all in all, John has finally settled down and found happiness. He lives in San Diego with his family and publishes a very successful TV-entertainment magazine. People told him it wasn't a very good business idea to take on TV Guide. But John did anyway and he's made it work. One thing you never want to tell John Rodgers is that he can't do something. He's overcome way too many odds to believe something like that.

Chapter twenty-two

*It was difficult,
in a way, to tell
several people*

I felt we had the finest coaching staff in the country and when it came time for me to quit, I was asked to recommend a successor. I had worked with all our coaches for 11 years — either as a player or a coach — and some of the others, such as John Melton and Carl Selmer, for 16 years. I had known Mike since 1935 and Jim since 1946. I had to make a choice.

I picked Tom Osborne to succeed me as head football coach because I felt he had the best chance of doing the job. I've said many times since then that I think Tom is the best football coach in the country; I honestly do believe that. If I were going to have a college team or a pro team, I'd rather have Tom coach it than any other coach, at any level. I knew Tom was the guy for this job, but it wasn't an easy thing to name him. There were pressures from other parts of the university as to who would be the most qualified for this job, and I know we'd have had problems getting some of the people who were being recommended, okayed by the Board of Regents. But as I just said, that wasn't the reason I picked Tom. I felt he was the one for the job.

I made that decision over a period of time. I used to talk to Jim Ross about it. Jim and I have known each other and been very close for a lot of years. Jim is one of Tom's biggest fans, too, as far as his being the head coach. It was a difficult thing, but I knew, as an athletic director, it was something I should do. Tom and I never went out and drank together or did other foolish things. I associated with Tom mostly in coaching situations and I have the utmost respect for him both on and off the football field. He and I don't always think alike on some subjects. Our attitudes about life are also different in some ways. But I knew he was a good person and that he would never get us into any trouble. You always knew he'd go right down the middle of the road as far as the rules were concerned.

In some ways it was a gradual decision. The more I watched Tom coach and the more I was around him, the more I felt he would have the best chance for success. I had known most of the other coaches for a long time, and I thought any one of them would have been very satisfactory as a head coach. They would have done a good job, but I thought there was one thing about Tom being the coach — he had a great offensive mind, one of the greatest I've ever seen.

Tom really started to work a lot with our offense after the 1968 season. We started running out of the I-formation and the spread in 1969 because we felt teams were catching up to our unbalanced line and we needed to get out of it. We were running a little bit of both, balanced and unbalanced, and it was tough to teach them both. Besides, the defenses seemed to know how to play us; they'd overshift to the short side to stop the run and then they'd overshift the defensive backfield to the long side so that they'd have our passing game pretty well stopped. That's when we got interested in the I-formation. It looked like a pretty good offense, so we started to study it. We went to coaching clinics. We got some of our ideas from John McKay at Southern Cal, who had used the 'I' for several years. We really went to work on it, and we also came up with the spread offense. It was a little different spread from the older formation, where the ends were wide and the two halfbacks were outside the tackles.

About that same time, we made another change, too. Tom Osborne was put in the press box. I felt he was the guy we wanted to help call the plays. Tom could analyze things up in the press box very well. When we'd get in a long-yardage situation, we'd call Tom. If we didn't make much on first down, before the next play, we'd tell him to be alert for something in case we were still in a long-yardage situation on third down. He'd come up with the plays. For instance, on long-yardage downs, we started to run a lot of delays, where the end would block and then delay into an open spot inside the linebackers.

I've gotten away from what I was talking about there, but anyway, when I decided on Tom, I still felt an obligation to those other coaches, and I really felt the best way to keep them employed here was to hire Tom as the head coach. I talked to Tom about keeping them, and he was in agreement about that; he's done it faithfully.

I began thinking about stepping down as head coach in 1969. I considered not coaching any more and, at one point, had decided the 1971 season would be my last. Nobody had ever won three straight national championships, and after we won our second in the '71 season, that prompted me to say I'd like to coach one more year and give it a try. At that time I had turned more of the coaching over to the other staff members. I wasn't quite as involved in it as back when I first started coaching. I gave it a lot of thought, though, believe me. I was thinking very seriously about retiring after both the 1970 and 1971 seasons. Each year I reconsidered. The thought of winning three straight national championships kept me going.

The main reason I had started thinking about retiring in

1969 was that it was all getting to be kind of a hassle. I had become the athletic director in May of 1967, when Tippy Dye left, and I just felt like the two jobs were quite a bit more work than doing either one of them, separately. Also, I had lost a little interest in the recruiting part of college coaching. My last real hard recruiting years were 1968-69. But actually, I didn't do really as much recruiting the last couple of years as I had before. The rest of the staff did a lot more of it than I did. Besides fall football and recruiting we had winter conditioning and spring practice. I was getting tired of it all, because to be a good football coach these days, you have to work very hard the whole year round.

I talked to Tom about the coaching situation during that time, and after the 1971 season, I got together with him and said: "Tom, I'd like to try this one more year." That's when we made him assistant head coach. Incidentally, to go along with his coaching ability, Tom is and was an excellent recruiter. Carl Selmer wanted the job as head coach very badly. And Carl was a fine football coach. However, the thing I felt about Carl was, he would always find out what was wrong with something and why it wouldn't work. But seldom did Carl come up with the answers or offensive ideas of his own. And this bothered me some as far as Carl becoming the head coach. In the minds of some people, most especially his own, Carl was Tom's main competition for the job. There were people who thought he should get the job, too. He is a fine coach. He impressed people with his intelligence. I hated to see Carl leave Nebraska. But I know he was very disappointed — and thought if he moved he might have a better chance to get a head coaching job. He went to Miami of Florida as assistant to Pete Elliott and later did become the head coach at Miami.

After I had made my decision to pick Tom, I had to tell the rest of my staff. I told those on the staff who were in town. Then I went back to my office to call Mike Corgan. Mike was gone at the time. As one of my oldest friends, I called him long distance to let him know I had chosen Tom. It wasn't easy, believe me. I think Mike felt real bad about

My family! Next to me, Phyllis, daughter Pat, daughter-in-law Cheri Jo, and son Mike.

it. I think John Melton felt bad, too.

I don't really know how they all feel about it now. I think I know how some of them feel, but there are others I'm not sure of. John Melton, for instance, was extremely loyal to me and he's been an extremely loyal assistant to Tom. John, who is a fine recruiter, incidentally, has been very, very good about the whole thing. Well, really, they've all been extremely loyal, and I think, or at least I hope, they believe in their own minds that I made the right choice, that Tom was the man for the job. Even Carl has been more friendly to me since he's been away from here than he ever was before. He probably hates to admit it, but I think even he might have realized by now that we made the right choice when we hired Tom Osborne.

It was also difficult, in a way, to tell people like Clete Fischer, who is a very fine coach and had been around the program for a long time. An interesting thing about Fischer was, when we first came here, Cliff Hardin, the chancellor, asked me, "Bob, there's one guy on this staff that I'd like you to keep for at least one year." That was Clete Fischer. Clete had just come from Midland High School in Texas. He'd been here only one year. Cliff must have made some promise to Clete when he came up here, so I said: "Sure, that's fine with me." Then we decided to keep George Kelly, too. George was a very gregarious fellow and a good football coach. After the first year, we definitely wanted Clete and George on our staff, so we kept 'em both. We've always felt that way about Clete; he's been very loyal and very good for this football program. George Kelly left here to go to Notre Dame prior to the 1969 season, after we had those two 6-4 records. I kidded him and told him he was leaving a sinking ship. I said: "George, you just want to get back to that Golden Dome before we go under."

A little story about George, after he left here for Notre Dame, one of our people stopped to visit him in South Bend one or two summers later. George was all excited about the place, you know, the tradition and all, and he said it was so much different at Notre Dame than it had been at Nebraska, what with all the talent Notre Dame was able to recruit. George supposedly said that some of the players who started at Nebraska probably would have trouble making the travel squad at Notre Dame, that's how much talent there was. Well, that was before we played Notre Dame in the Orange Bowl following the 1972 season. After we had beaten them 40-6, this guy went over to George and kind of rubbed it in. He said: "George, I was wondering, which of our starters do you think couldn't have made Notre Dame's travel squad?"

George has always been a position coach at Notre Dame. I don't know what positions he's working with now, but he's never been a defensive coordinator. George probably had a better job here than he does there, and I think he might even have gotten paid more here than he's getting at Notre Dame. But George's wife, Gloria, is from that area and so is George. He played at Notre Dame. I would have moved, too, if I had been in George's situation. George and I have always remained friends. He is a great guy.

Dan Devine, who coached at Notre Dame, called me one time. I hadn't heard from him in about six years and he called me on the phone one day and told me they were going to dedicate a building at Michigan State to Duffy Daugherty. He wanted to know if I knew that. I said: "No, and I appreciate your calling to tell me." But he didn't hang up then; he talked and talked, for a long time. He didn't sound real good, you know; it sounded like he was grasping for something, but I don't know what and there wasn't any way I could say anything to help. Dan had some problems, some of which he created for himself and some of which haven't been his fault. Coaching at Notre Dame can be a real pressure-packed situation.

Once I picked Tom Osborne and Tom became the head coach, I tried to step out of the picture. I resolved not to interfere in Tom's business, which is sometimes difficult for a guy who had coached as long as I had. But I had seen how Iowa had problems when Forrest Evashevski quit coaching and became athletic director. Some of the coaches who worked under Evy told me that at times there was interference and none of them lasted very long. Evy was a great player and a great coach, but he might have quit coaching too soon for him to completely divorce himself from coaching.

And, as I said before, I also saw what had happened at Michigan State. Duffy Daughtery became the coach when Biggie Munn retired from coaching and became the athletic director. At one time, Biggie and Duffy were just like brothers. But when Biggie appointed Duffy head coach, the problems began. Biggie second guessed Duffy, and I could see the bitterness begin to grow. I saw how Duffy felt, and the terrible problem that was created. I made up my mind that once I got out of coaching, that would be it for me. I have never offered Tom a suggestion of any kind. We've talked about things in general, but not about anything that pertained to his coaching.

Speaking of coaching associations and situations in which I was involved, I'll tell you a guy who was a fine football coach, Lloyd Eaton. I don't really know why Lloyd ever left Northern Michigan, where he was the head coach, to come out to Wyoming and be an assistant coach for me. I could never quite figure that out. When I asked him if he wanted to join us, I was surprised that he said he would. Also, at that time, when I was putting together my Wyoming staff, I did something which I realize now was real unethical though at the time I didn't think about that. Today, I would have. Anyway, I asked John Tobin if he would be interested in going to Wyoming. John was an assistant coach for Frank Waters at Hillsdale College, and I asked him even though I hadn't contacted Frank first. I never did talk to Frank until after John had decided he wanted to come. That was bad.

Eddie Crowder didn't talk to me about his talking to Tom Osborne when there was talk of Tom going out to Colorado a couple of years ago. See, Eddie pulled the same thing I did when I talked to John Tobin about going to Wyoming. Eddie didn't mention it to me until later, after

I'll sign if it isn't a blank check.

the discussions were already in the works. Tom didn't talk to me immediately either when they first contacted him, but I believe that when they originally contacted him, Tom wasn't much interested in the job. In fact, I don't think he figured it was necessary because he didn't think the job was something he'd ever take. Then, a group of his assistant coaches, especially the newer ones, said: "Let's look into it first before we say we're not interested." Anyway, those people might have gotten to Tom a little. And, at the time, I think Tom was pretty bitter about the Orange Bowl and how we'd been forced to play a rematch with Oklahoma down there after we had beaten them during the regular season. Tom might have been a little upset about the criticism he had received, and then he had some problems with his TV show at that time. Things had just started piling up. That's the best way to put it; Tom might have had a feeling that he wasn't appreciated much around here, and that, I think, brought people to their senses, about not wanting to lose Tom. Fortunately, though, that whole incident served a purpose because ever since then, people have appreciated Tom Osborne more. That's pretty obvious.

As I was saying, though, Lloyd Eaton was a fine coach, a real fine football coach, and I'll tell you, among the assistant coaches who worked at Michigan State, Earle Edwards was a good one. Earle was one of the finest coaches I've ever seen, anyplace. He helped me a tremendous amount while I was at Michigan State, and even when I first came here. Steve Sebo was another assistant at Michigan State who was a good football coach. Steve went to Pennsylvania, and I guess you could say he sort of flunked a course there, but he's been various places and he's done a good job. Steve was a backfield coach. Earle went to North Carolina State and just turned that program around. Wimp Hewgley, a young guy we tried to get to come with us to Nebraska but who stayed with Lloyd Eaton at Wyoming, was another good young coach; he played for us our first year at Wyoming.

Now, you talk about good football coaches who are

known all around the country, well, Bear Bryant is a fine football coach. He's still a good leader, and he's been successful everywhere he's coached. He had success at Kentucky. He had success at Texas A&M, and he's had success at Alabama, so he has to be a tremendous football coach. I guess the only time I resented Bear Bryant's popularity was when he was picked Coach of the Year after we had beaten Alabama, 38-6, in the 1972 Orange Bowl and I had a 13-0 record. That wasn't Bear's fault and he actually voted for me. The problem may have been that year they were voting for Coach of the Year before the bowl games. After that year they changed the rules and now the vote is taken after the bowl games.

To the Alabama people, Bear is legendary figure. They think he can do anything, and you certainly can't find anybody around that university who will say even one bad thing about Bear Bryant. Of course, I've always felt that assistant coaches were pretty important to a program, too, that it can never be just one guy doing the job. But in Alabama, they think it's Bear Bryant doing all the work.

I don't think Coach Bryant gets up in his tower any more. He rides out to the field in a golf cart. I've been on the tower with him a couple of times, and the last time I was there, he introduced me around to his players and told them how bad we beat Alabama in the Orange Bowl that last year. To me, personally, Bear Bryant has always been a good friend and a great coach and I don't have any arguments with him or what he does. I hope he will become the winningest coach as this book is published.

There are other coaches I've run into that I've thought were good coaches and people who I respect. Chuck Fairbanks was a good football coach at Oklahoma, and he still is a good one. I've known Chuck for a long time. Everybody makes so many mistakes in a lifetime, and I think one of Chuck's biggest was to go to Colorado from New England. Chuck was very discouraged at Colorado. I talked to him not long ago, after another one of his players had quit on him, and he was very down. I tried to help him get his chin up a little bit because I've known the guy and coached against him in college. I wanted to cheer him up.

Then there are guys like Frank Kush, who I think is a good coach, and Bud Wilkinson, people who I've been associated with ... Bud and I have always been friendly, even before I came into the Big Eight. Bud Wilkinson was a real good friend of Duffy Daugherty, and he used to come back to Michigan State once in awhile. I remember one spring, Duffy, Bill Yeoman, Lou Agase and I drove down to watch Oklahoma's spring practice. That was quite a trip. I've known Bud Wilkinson for a long time, and I have great respect for him as a coach.

I worked for two very fine football coaches at Michigan State — Biggie Munn and Duffy Daugherty. I only worked for Biggie one year, but I had great respect for him. Duffy and I have been friends for many years. Duffy had two real strong points besides being a good all-around coach. One was his ability to react on the field the day of a game, and his ability to recruit. Bud Wilkinson once said, "Next to Jesus Christ, Duffy may have been the world's best recruiter."

As far as professional coaches, I've met them and I know a little bit about some of them but not enough to make judgments on them. You know, I'd hate to say whether Tom Landry is a better football coach than, say, Don Shula. I just don't know that much about those people. But as far as guys who have coached in college, Johnny McKay was a fine college coach and I'm sure he's a very good professional coach, too. I think a big part of being recognized as a very successful coach, is being in the right place at the right time. That's vitally important. For instance, I think that was part of the reason I was successful right away at Nebraska. I came into a situation at the right time, because the people here wanted to win so badly and we inherited a fairly good bunch of football players. It's like I've said before, I talked to one of the coaches who was here before we came, following that 1962 season when we won nine games and went to the Gotham Bowl, and I told him: "If you guys had stayed here another year with this bunch of kids, the same success would have happened to you." He said: "No, it wouldn't have." You know, they had lost confidence and thought they had a bad organization.

chapter twenty-three

*I learned at an early age
to watch out for all that crap
in the newspapers*

When I was growing up in Saginaw, I had a newspaper route in one of the poorest sections of the city. Most of my customers lived in tenement buildings or what were known as cold water flats. A lot of them didn't even have indoor plumbing. They had to use chamber pots instead. You can understand how that wouldn't always be a real pleasant experience, being in the same room with a used chamber pot. Well, these people were poor, but they weren't stupid. They came up with their own sewage disposal system. They'd empty the waste in their newspapers and wrap it up. Then, early in the mornings about the time I was delivering my papers, these people would throw their newspapers out the window. You could say I learned at an early age to watch out for all that crap in the newspapers.

Actually, some of my best friends over the years have been sportswriters. The first year I was in Lincoln, Don Bryant was sports editor of The Lincoln Star, Dick Becker was sports editor of The Lincoln Journal and Wally Provost was sports editor of The Omaha World-Herald. Bryant, of course, is now one of my assistant athletic directors and the sports information director at Nebraska. Becker is the head man at Ak-Sar-Ben. Bryant is, in my opinion, the greatest sports information director in the business, and Becker has done a great job at Ak-Sar-Ben. Provost is still the World-Herald's No. 1 columnist.

They'd probably deny it now, but I bet no sportswriter leaped up and did jumping jacks when I was hired. The program was in the doldrums and the writers had to endure a lot of the frustration. If they were a little skeptical watching me come in, I really couldn't blame 'em. I would have been skeptical, too.

It wasn't really a conscious effort at the time to try and win over the media. But I will admit I went out of my way to make them feel welcome and comfortable. The best way I could think to do it was with a little humor.

Sometimes during practice, when things were under control, I'd go over to the sidelines and shoot the bull with the press. We'd tell jokes and everyone would laugh. It took the pressure off.

I'd take an ordinary story and relate it to football. Usually, it would deal about the intelligence of our athletes.

One of the stories I'd use was about this kid we were recruiting in Pennsylvania. I went into his home and noticed one of his ears was gone. So I said: "Harold, what happened to your ear?"

And he said: "You know, I was pressing my pants and the phone rang. Instead of answering the phone, I put the iron to my ear."

So I said: "But Harold, your other ear's gone, too."

And he said: "Yeah, wouldn't you know — the son of a gun called back."

Another standard was the one about the coaching staff trying to decide who was the dumbest player on the team. This became a matter of considerable debate and neither coach could convince the other what player was the dumbest.

About that time, one of the players walks by the office. Jim Ross would wink at me and say he was going to show me how dumb Fred was.

He'd say: "Hey Fred, there's something I want you to do. Take this dime out on West O Street and buy me a new car, would ya?"

Old Fred would take the dime, put it in his pocket and say, "Okay, coach."

About the time I'd think I was losing the argument, Willie would walk by. So I decided to use the same strategy.

I'd say: "Willie, there's something I want you to do. Take this dime out on campus and find a pay telephone. When you do, call my office and see if I'm in."

Willie would take the dime, put it in his pocket and say, "Okay, coach."

Well, Fred and Willie meet out in front of the Coliseum and they start talking about how dumb their coaches are. Naturally, they can't decide who's the dumbest.

Fred nominates Jim Ross. "You know what he just did?" he'd ask. "He just gave me a dime and told me to go out on West O Street and buy him a new car. Shoot, he's so dumb, he didn't even tell me what color he wanted."

Then Willie would say: "If you think that's dumb, what about Coach Devaney? You know what he just did? He told me to take a dime, find a pay telephone and call his office to see if he was in. For crying out loud, the phone was right next to him. He could have called himself."

Then there was this one recruit. He told us that he was so poor, every time his mother tossed the dog a bone, he had to signal for a fair catch or the other kids would beat him to it.

I know they're silly stories. But a punch line will loosen you up. Sometimes, a good punch line can be more than a joke. It can be pretty realistic. One I used early at Nebraska still holds true for Tom Osborne today. I used to tell luncheon groups and banquet audiences that "I know you-'re with me all the way — win or tie." It always got a laugh, probably because everyone knew it was true.

That first year I was here, we all needed to laugh. We wanted to forget about the past and be positive about the future. We wanted the players to think as positively as a 90-year-old man who marries a 20-year-old woman and buys a five-bedroom house near an elementary school.

We were so busy selling our program and ourselves in the early years that we were always either coaching, recruiting or speaking somewhere.

The media helped us spread the word. Bryant and Becker can tell you all about the Gotham Bowl because they were there. I knew that first year that this was a good newspaper state because they'd spend whatever it took to be wherever they needed to be.

I owed a big debt to Gregg McBride of The Omaha World-Herald. When I first got here, the newspaper guys knew how to pronounce my name. But the radio and TV guys kept calling me "Duh-vain-ee." It kind of aggravated me, but I didn't want to make a big deal of it. Finally, McBride wrote a column and said Devaney rhymed with fanny. He said it about three or four times for emphasis. He got the point across. That was the last time I had a problem with the media knowing how to pronounce my name.

Things weren't always perfect with the media, though. I had a little run-in with one writer in 1969. He interviewed the players about who they wanted to succeed me and did a big spread on it. I told him it would be a good idea to find out when I was going to get out of coaching first. It made me a little mad, but I got over it. It's hard to complain about the coverage football gets in this state. If you read every story, by the time the season's over, you know everything about every starter except what time of the day he went to the bathroom.

Writers who came to practice every day knew what was

going on. They had eyes and ears. If they didn't see it, they'd hear about it. They were competitive and they did great jobs. But they still got along personally. I enjoyed my friendships with Conde Sargent, Hal Brown and Don Forsythe. They all lived in Lincoln, but Conde wrote for the World-Herald. Forsythe and Brown were the guys who succeeded Becker and Bryant on the Lincoln papers.

I had other associations with sportswriters. Volney Meece of the Oklahoma City Times, Maury White of the Des Moines Register and Charlie Smith, who was working for UPI out of Kansas City, are friends. So are John Mooney of the Salt Lake City Tribune, Fred Russell of the Nashville Banner and Chet Nelson of the Rocky Mountain News. I enjoyed reading Joe McGuff in the Kansas City Star. Those guys and every other sportswriter were always welcome to watch us practice.

Somebody asked me once why I had such an open door to practices. They asked me why I wasn't worried about someone stealing secrets and sharing them with the enemy. My answer was simple. I said if we didn't know what we were doing, I sure as hell didn't think anybody else could figure it out. That's why I did coaching clinics in states like Kansas. I shared what I knew. If KU and K-State picked up on it, that was their problem.

I still remember the famous spy story that surfaced in the newspapers after our win over Oklahoma in the 1971 Game of the Century. Some writer interviewed an Oklahoma guy who said he spent all week at our practices.

He said he lived in the men's room in the East Stadium and charted all our plays during practice. The media wanted me to respond. All I said was it must have been pretty stinky, living all week in a john. I also said the guy must not have been too smart for two reasons: (1) Oklahoma didn't win; and (2) our practices were open all week. He should have sat in the stands. He would have been a lot more comfortable ... and he might have smelled a little better, too.

Newspapers like a little humor in their copy. I guess be-

The Bob Devaney and Bill Russell Morning Show? Not really, but we had a good time.

cause I was willing to give them some, they were willing to forgive my bad grammar. I'd use don't when I should have used doesn't or mix up the tense of a few verbs now and then. But the writers never had to guess where I was coming from. I never tightened my lip at Nebraska. My attitude always has been that the media is important. They're the link to all the fans. You don't realize how much the fans read until you talk to 'em. That's when you learn how they form their opinions. I decided a long time ago that if the media is that powerful, you might as well make it as interesting and as informative as you can.

I did agonize about one thing. When we started winning and going to the big bowls, I worried about my players popping off in the locker room and saying something that an opponent could use against us. I wondered if it was smart for writers to be in the locker room right after a ball game. I just knew that sometime, in the exhilaration of a big win, someone was going to say something that would wind up on someone else's bulletin board. I didn't like the idea of stepping on the press or censuring my players. But if it was going to be the difference in a big game, I thought it might be best to change the interview policy. I don't know why I changed my mind. I guess I decided it hadn't cost us in the past and it wasn't worth worrying about it costing us in the future.

I'm glad I figured that out. It probably wouldn't have hurt much during the great years. But it might have caused some problems when we went 6-4 in '67 and '68. By that time, I'd decided we could explain a loss just as well as we could analyze a win. Really, when you think about it, that's the way it should be. These coaches who say their players can't talk to the press after a game aren't showing much respect for their players or their fans. Colorado even had a coach who said his players weren't available after a loss because they suffered enough on the field. It's not easy, I know. With the media, you either love 'em or hate 'em. There seems to be no in between. But if coaches have learned anything, they should have learned that alienation doesn't do much for anyone.

I've always felt in this business, you have to take the bad with the good. National writers always took kindly to our program, but they rarely described me in very respectable terms. I remember Time magazine calling me "a paunchy, puffy-eyed Irishman." Newsweek said I was pudgy and didn't match the new breed of college football coaches. They said Ara Parseghian, John McKay and Darrell Royal were suave and I was more like Wallace Beery than Kirk Douglas. Then they said I was 10 years older than I was.

My wife had the clippings, but I never read 'em until after I got out of coaching, so I didn't know they were cutting me up at the time.

I do remember a writer coming to Lincoln from back East. He took one look at my wardrobe and called me the poor man's version of Willy Loman. He said I had a unique blend of colors and a unique way for my clothes to fit. Sports Illustrated asked me if I'd read the story. I said no, but I was furious. "Tell that guy I'm going to sue him and his magazine for defamation," I said. Then I had to smile.

"Of course," I said, "he will be able to offer the perfect defense — the truth."

I got a lot of mileage out of that whole thing. Everybody chided me about my lack of style. I told the Nebraska writers I didn't mind. The only thing that made me feel bad was that writer seeing me in my best suit.

I didn't mind, really. That writer didn't have much style either. He drank a lot while he was out here doing the story. And it was mostly my liquor. But a terrible thing happened. After he wrote the story, he died. They cremated him and it took three days to put out the fire.

John Underwood of Sports Illustrated liked that kind of humor. John's another friend in the media, even if he did write one time that I had a broad pleasant potato face and a dumpy baker's build. I didn't like his description, but he was telling the truth, too.

No matter what the press said, I always considered it an

ally, not an enemy. When I was coaching, the media had a good sense of humor. They were looking for a laugh as much as they were looking for a good story. Of course, the times were different. The intellectual snobs were calling us football factories, but that big black cloud of cheating wasn't hanging over everyone's head.

You could joke about things back then that you can't joke about now. When I first came to Nebraska, I made a remark that made everyone laugh. I told the press: "I don't expect to win enough games to be put on NCAA probation. I just want to win enough to warrant an investigation."

Everyone sort of picked up on that. It made some national magazines and there wasn't anyone who didn't see it as kind of funny. Nowadays, of course, that kind of statement would have too much shock value. People would probably take you seriously. They'd see it as a cause for investigation.

The media can be an important part of recruiting. What they say leaves an imprint. If they take you on, they can make you look worse than you are. Of course, they can make you look better than you are, too.

The most popular recruiting story I ever had was the one I told earlier about Tony Jeter. He lived in West Virginia and was all set to go to Arizona State. I decided to drop by his house anyway — just about the time his mother was sitting down to play the organ. I sat down with her and sang a few hymns. I remember one of them was "Bringing in the Sheaves." Tony told the newspapers that once his mamma heard my Irish tenor, there was never a doubt where he was going to college. He was coming to Nebraska to play for that nice Mr. Devaney.

It was a great story, but people started applying it to everyone. One reporter asked me if I sat down and sang hymns with a mother to get her son to come to Nebraska. I said: "Yes, I did that. The mother came to Nebraska and the boy enrolled at Missouri." It helped break up the monotony of the story.

I was lucky. Most of my good lines went over in the me-

I think I was about to say something funny. Or was it the other Bob?

dia. But there were a couple that caused me some grief.

The one everyone heard about was right after we beat LSU in the Orange Bowl to win our first national championship. I guess I couldn't leave well enough alone. Texas was No. 1 and Notre Dame knocked them off in the Cotton Bowl. Even though Notre Dame had lost a game, Ara Parseghian lobbied that they should be No. 1 because they accepted a greater challenge than Nebraska did in the Orange Bowl.

Well, that was a bunch of crap, so I made the remark that "not even the Pope could vote for Notre Dame." Parseghian jumped on it and said it was in poor taste. I'd done something I didn't intend to do — rile up all the Catholics. I was afraid Ara's comments might influence the vote, but the writers were too smart to take some coach's word. Coaches don't know anything about rankings anyway.

Unfortunately, I didn't learn from that mistake. In 1972, we got tied at Iowa State, 23-23. We were horrible. I said we played like a bunch of farmers at a picnic. The farmers thought I was making fun of them. I was talking more about the picnic than the farmers. I could have said laborers, shoe clerks, anything and no one would have cared.

The next week we beat Kansas State, 59-7, for my 100th win at Nebraska. Afterwards, I said we played like a bunch of farmers at harvest time. That was okay. I guess winning has something to do with your perspective.

chapter twenty-four

He may be a millionaire,
but my good friend Cappy
was a shrewd one at Alma

If I wrote a book and didn't include a word about F.L. (Francis Leo) Cappaert, he'd probably be happy. Cappy is one of my closest friends. But he isn't much for publicity. He never has been and never will be. Most people around the Nebraska program know he's a self-made millionaire, but he's always been a little bit of a mystery man, too. He's always been cordial with the press, but every time anyone tried to write a story on him, he kind of backed off. One of the most interesting guys I've ever known had a great story to tell, but never told it. He didn't think business stories belonged on the sports pages.

Well, he may be right about that. But I've decided that if I didn't tell the F.L. Cappaert Story, my book just wouldn't be complete. Cappy and I go back a long, long way.

He comes from Clare, Michigan. It's about the size of a Class C town in Nebraska, located about 28 miles from

Alma in North Central Michigan. I first met him at Alma College. He was a freshman when I was a senior. We both lived in the school gymnasium that year. There were two rooms at the end of the gym, one in each corner, two double bunkbeds in each room. We got to know each other real well, even though he was a young freshman and I was an old senior. I was a 170-pound end and he was a 185-pound fullback. He was more a blocker than he was a ball carrier. He was a tough kid and I think he looked up to me because I was somewhat like him.

Cappy looked up to me, not because I was an all-conference football player or captain of the team, but because I was the heavyweight boxing champion at Alma. You've got to remember it was 1939 when we met. Boxing was a pretty big thing in those days. There were boxing clubs in a lot of the high schools in Michigan and boxing clubs in many of the colleges. Cappy took a liking to me because I didn't want to box in the medium weights at Alma. You could always move up a class, but never down. I decided I'd go for heavyweight or nothing. I was from the streets, so I thought I was pretty tough. I wanted to show people I could give out punishment as well as it take it. When I won the heavyweight championship, I became Cap's friend. He didn't think anyone was going to try and cross me and get away with it.

Cap was also the student manager for a very good basketball team. I mean, in those days Alma could play with Michigan, Michigan State or just about anybody in basketball. Cap was in charge of all the meal money. I always accused him of buying everyone hamburgers and pocketing the extra money for himself. Even today, I tell him that's how he got his start on the way to his first million. I told that so much, people started to believe me. But honestly, Cappy was a pretty shrewd operator. I also used to say that whenever his restaurant income was slipping, he'd make the players wear their sweat socks until they had holes in 'em . . . while he sold the new ones for a profit. You could kid Cap like that and he'd laugh right along with you.

When I got out of college, Cap and I sort of lost track of each other. He ended up joining the Navy after college and became a PT boat commander. He was involved in a lot of combat in the Pacific. When he got out, he started gambling in the business world in the 1950s. He did a little bit of everything. Cappaert Enterprises was a corporation with more than 60 companies all over the United States and all over the world. He was involved in truck lines, cattle, electronics, towing. He even had a big barge company that unloaded ships in Kuwait and some of those countries. Cap was a millionaire sometime in his early thirties. He had about $4 million before anyone really heard of him. The company that made him was Gurden Industries, a mobile home company headquartered in Louisville. He made his biggest fortune in one stroke of the pen. He started that company in 1951 and worked his butt off, morning, noon and night. Finally, it got to be too much for an old country boy like Cap. He decided it was time to let someone else run it. He finally sold it in 1967 for about $50 million. Sometimes, he'd wake up in the middle of the night, wishing he had the company back. Then he'd wake up in the morning and realize he'd made the right move. By that time, he was pretty diversified. Everything he touched was turning to gold.

Some national magazine — I'm not sure if it was Fortune or what — listed Cap as one of the 10 richest self-made millionaires in the world. They estimated his wealth from as low as $100 million to as high as $300 million. I never really asked Cap which figure was closest to the truth. He would have told me it didn't make any difference — knowing that, plus 15 cents, would buy you a cup of coffee. I don't know if Cap knew how wealthy he was, or even cared. He just wanted to enjoy himself. More than just about anything else, he loves football and airplanes. Cap was a good athlete and I kept up with him while he was still going to Alma. So he kept up with me when I started

My Alma College buddy, Cap, and our coaching staff. That's
Cap's plane we're boarding.

coaching. He'd come to our games when I was an assistant at Michigan State. When I went to Wyoming, he showed up the week we played Air Force in 1959. We had a helluva football team, but just played terrible that day. We should have beaten the dickens out of Air Force, but that was the only game we lost that year. That night, we took Cap and his wife out to dinner with all the coaches and their wives. Everybody in Laramie went to the Elks Club to celebrate on Saturday night. We were all disappointed, but we decided to have a good time anyway. I'll never forget how surprised Cap was to see all of us unwind. He said if we were this happy when we lost, he'd hate like hell to be around us when we won.

Cap would fly up to Wyoming for games, but it was a tough flight from Vicksburg, Mississippi, to Laramie. Cap had mostly piston planes in those days. When we went to Nebraska, he started showing up for every game because it was easier to get there and he had his own Air Force by then. With the faster planes, he could get to Lincoln in a couple hours. The best airplane he had was a BAC (British Aircraft Corporation) One-Eleven jet. It was a little bigger than a DC-9 and was designed to seat 82 passengers. But Cap converted it into an executive plane that seated 22. I think it cost him $3½ million. The same plane today would cost $8 or $9 million.

Anyway, it was costing Cap $1 million dollars a year just to run it. He had a crew of four — two pilots, a maintainence man and his own chef, John Pierre, who's now a chef for the French Embassy in Washington. Every year, Cap would take the coaches' wives on a road trip and they loved John Pierre. Cap would fly one of his smaller jets to wherever we were playing on Friday, so he could stay with the team on Friday nights. On Saturday mornings, John Pierre would meet the coaches' wives, pin a big flower on 'em and have a big brunch waiting. He'd fix these big fancy salads and all those fancy pastries and desserts. He was exceptional. After the games, he'd fix steaks, vegetables and all the sauces that go with good French food. You've heard of gourmet tailgate parties at football games. But no one in the world could match John Pierre. He was the best.

Of course, he worked on a plane that had everything. It had a big deep freeze, air-conditioning, the whole bit. There was a snack bar for candies and peanuts, a wet bar and a refrigeration bar. There was a big table that seated five or six people, a circular couch for another five or six, a dining area and another area where you could play cards. It had a crew's quarters, a big bathroom, even a bedroom with a big circular bed. But he was too much of a businessman to use the bed. When he flew on the plane, he was always on the telephone next to his special seat. He had an electric type-writer and conducted his business right there on the plane. Sometimes, he'd make business trips where he didn't even get out of the plane. His partners would rather meet him at the airport and conduct business where there was good food and comfortable chairs.

Cap's plane was a forerunner to the plush, modern exec-utive plane. People tried to copy it. Cap told people if he had it to do over, he'd go without the bed. He'd always say if you can't stay up six or seven hours, you shouldn't get on the plane anyway. It was a luxury suited to others more than him. Cap had a ground lease on the plane and I know Sonny and Cher used it once for one of their tours. Elvis Presley and his wife also used it. Cap donated it to Richard Nixon the first time he ran for president and he used it to campaign.

Cap was a good Republican and there were a few times when I was almost guilty by association. His name surfaced once as a contributor to the Nebraska Finance Committee to Re-elect the President. I think he donated $3,000, the same amount Howard Hughes donated to the same fund.

That reminds me of another story. Cap and Hughes weren't on speaking terms, but their business people dealt with each other. Cap talked to Bob Maheu, the guy who tried to sue Hughes' for $16 million. Right when Hughes was really getting into the casino business big, Cap wanted to build a tramway that would take passengers from the

Las Vegas Airport and let them off at their hotels on the strip, then go downtown. It was a hell of an idea and Hughes' people thought about going in with him. But it never came off because of the unions of cab drivers and all that. Hell, you'd have to shoot them first. Someday, Cap thinks the idea will come to pass anyway.

You wouldn't get some members of our coaching staff, or me, to dispute something Cap suggests. He's brought me in on a couple of business things that turned out okay. I've made some bad business decisions in my life, but not with Cap. He took over a company called El Pak when it went bankrupt and turned it into a real going outfit. He had four or five million shares that he bought from 25 cents to a dollar a share. By the time he sold it in the mid-seventies, he got $10 to $12 a share. A lot of our coaches bought shares in the same company. Joe Cipriano said he put his kid through college selling his stock in the company. It went up as high as $50, then split. The company is called New Park now and it's about $25 a share. Some of our coaches got out and made some money at $4 or $5 a share. Some got out at $10 or $12. Some are still holding their stock in the company. It's been good for everybody.

Cap has been very generous to our football program. He had a G-1 turbo-prop that seated about 14. He took our whole coaching staff to the college all-star game when we played the Dallas Cowboys in Chicago. When we played at Army in 1972, he took all the coaches' wives to New York. He loves football, whether you're playing in a Wyoming blizzard or under a hot sun in Honolulu. You can always count on Cap being there. He'll drop whatever he's doing. Once, he was in Turkey, but made it to Lincoln by kickoff. Another time, he was doing business in Israel. He wasn't quite finished, but he left anyway. He's almost like an assistant coach. If Cap wasn't there, you felt like something was missing.

Cap never worries about the weather. He has so many homes, he just goes wherever he needs to go. If it's too hot in Mississippi, he goes to Michigan. If it's too cold in Michigan, he goes to Mississippi. I've always enjoyed his home about 6½ miles outside of Vicksburg. He has a big swimming pool in his pool house. It's about 40 by 45 feet, air-conditioned with a walk-in cooler, a walk-in deep freeze, a kitchen, pinball machines, slot machines, a pool table and a bar. Outside, there's a regulation-sized tennis court.

He used to spend most of his time in Vicksburg, but I suppose Cap spends just as much time in his hometown of Clare these days. He owns about 6,000 acres and has a gigantic house on a 102-acre lake. It's the only house on the lake. You can fish for bass and pike, but the relaxation is more fun than the fishing. You can go out there and get completely away from everything and everybody. Cap also has a big house in Baldwin, Michigan. A fresh water stream feeds into a real productive trout pond. Even I can catch trout there and pretend like I'm a fisherman. Cap is the type of guy who gets up every day and thinks it's going to be the best day of his life. He doesn't keep the Air Force he used to have. At one time, he owned six planes and three of 'em were jets. He doesn't own a pure jet anymore. He says fuel's too high and if it keeps going up, he's gonna get a mule, a buggy and join the Army. One thing about Cap. Despite all his wealth, he's still an old country boy. I've talked to people who've met him and they don't believe he's a millionaire. He'll probably be mad at me for describing all his luxuries. He's kept his life pretty private and I respect him for that. But I couldn't resist sharing a little more about a close friend.

Cap is one of the most devoted Nebraska football fans there is. He was with me when Richard Nixon came to Lincoln to honor the national championship team. Cap also enjoyed the night of my farewell dinner, when Joe Garagiola offered to come and be the main speaker for free. Then there was the night at another dinner in my honor when Lowell Thomas sat between us. I've never seen Cap so enthralled. He thought Lowell Thomas was one of the most remarkable men he'd ever met. It was a memorable night.

James Garner, an Oklahoma grad but an okay guy.

Cap never missed a game, not even a bowl game, while I coached at Nebraska. Even if it was the Hula Bowl, he'd be there. He still never misses a home game. He's a true fan. I remember in 1976, Cap was here for the Oklahoma game without his plane. At halftime, he got on the phone and ordered his plane to Lincoln, so we could check out the reservations in Miami that Sunday. That was the year Oklahoma beat us in the last minute with the flea-flicker play. The plane was already in the air. Cap couldn't have called it back if he'd wanted to. He didn't complain, though. He felt worse about the team and what they were going through. His heart was with them.

There are times when Cap wishes I was still coaching. He thinks I'd have been a good pro coach. If it hadn't been for a news leak, I might have had the chance. If I was ever going to coach pro football, I wanted a team down south where it was warm. Well, Cap thought about buying a team. He was interested in the New Orleans Saints. But before he ever had a chance to investigate, someone caught wind of it. The news leaked out of Vicksburg and everything was off before it had a chance to get started. I don't know what might have happened. I'm sure I would have had first crack at being his first head coach.

I'm glad it all fell through. I don't know if pro football would have been as much fun. They still call Cap "Go Big Red" in Vicksburg. I think Nebraska will be his favorite team the rest of his life.

chapter twenty-five

*I don't remember an official
or any single call against us
that ever cost us a ball game*

It's been claimed that I was always trying to psych the officials so they wouldn't call back any big play a team of mine made. Actually, there were certain officials I never said anything to. Like Vance Carlson. He was always going to do a good job — for both teams. You didn't need to try to kid around or say anything to him. There were a lot of other officials like that.

The only thing I used to try to do was to stay on them enough so that they knew that if they made a call I wasn't going to like, that they'd better be right. It kept them on their toes. But I was never penalized 15 yards in my entire career. I think that proves I was never abusive. But I tried to keep their attention. Some officials you had to keep their attention. If they were going to make a call against me, I wanted them to be darn sure they were positive about what they were doing.

The funny thing is, it was an official's call — which

worked out in our favor — that was the turning point in getting our long winning streak started. It happened in the Kansas game of 1969. We were 0-1 in league play — having lost to Missouri the week before — and we were 2-2 overall, having lost to Southern Cal in our opening game that year.

The Kansas game was the fifth game of the season. It was a home game in Lincoln. And we were losing! We were about to drop to 2-3 for the year and be in lots of trouble. Then we got that pass interference call. And, oh, Jeez, that was something.

The game was really a lost cause. We were beat. It was fourth and 18 or something like that. Our only chance was to complete a long pass. Well, Jim McFarland went down the field about 20 yards — enough for the first down — and hooked. The ball was thrown, but it was way high. He couldn't have reached it if he'd been on a ladder. But, before the ball got that far, a Kansas defender did interfere with McFarland — although it had no bearing on the play whatsoever. He'd have never been able to catch the pass if the guy had just left him alone. Hell, the ball was clear out of the park.

But the official on the play, all he does is see the Kansas guy pushing McFarland and he throws the flag. The question is, of course, should the official take into consideration where the ball was? But, anyway, he didn't, and down went the flag.

Emory Hicks, the Kansas captain, is mad as hell. He comes running over and remarks something about the ancestry of the official. Down goes another flag. They slap a 15-yard penalty on Hicks for unsportsmanlike conduct — on top of the distance of the interference call. Now, suddenly, we're getting close to the end zone.

Now, the entire Kansas team is really upset. On about the next play, somebody pops Guy Ingles and they get a half-the-distance-to-the-goal penalty. That's their third major penalty, one right on top of the other. And we score.

That started the string. We didn't lose again until after we'd won back-to-back national championships in 1970 and

'71. We went from that Kansas game, the fifth game of the 1969 season, until the opening game of the 1972 season — a last-second, 20-17, loss to UCLA — without losing.

Ironically, Pepper Rodgers was the opposing coach both times. He was coaching Kansas when the string started and he was coaching UCLA when it ended in Los Angeles.

That Kansas game was something, the way it turned around from what looked like a sure loss to a victory at the very end. Pepper was really upset. I don't blame him. I'd have been mad too. But those things happen. I remember the time we were playing Missouri in Lincoln. It was in 1968. We were behind, but our kids stopped them to force a punt. This would be our chance to win the ball game. We needed a good punt return. So what happens? Our players, who are back by the punt receiver to block for his return, are looking down field to see who to block and aren't aware of where the ball is. The punt is kicked short and the damn ball comes down and hits one of our guys on the top of his helmet. Missouri recovers and retains possession. That didn't happen just once. It happened twice in the same game. And Missouri recovered the ball both times. Two really key plays and we lost the game by two lousy points, 16-14. So I had some frustrating things happen to me too.

I don't remember, ever, an official — or any single call — that we felt ever really cost us a ball game. Although I sure remember a call that was going to beat us. It happened in the Orange Bowl game against Auburn after the 1963 season — my second year at Nebraska — which we won, 13-7. And that was a big victory for us in helping us get the program at Nebraska really turned around.

In those days, the officials for the bowl games were what they called "split crews." Half the officials came from each of the two conferences represented by the competing teams.

Toward the end of that game, Auburn had the ball near midfield. They were trying a bunch of long, desperation passes, hoping for a lucky touchdown catch or a pass interference call. We only had that six-point lead. A touchdown and the point after kick and we would be beaten.

Sure enough, one of the Southeastern Conference officials called a pass interference against us in the end zone. It was a terrible call. Our guy didn't interfere. We didn't even have a defender within three yards of the intended receiver. But the flag went down.

Well, before I can even get mad I saw one of the Big Eight officials drop his hankie for an offsetting penalty. He called Auburn for backfield in motion. That nullified the whole play.

I heard later that he told somebody, "I'll be damned if the Big Eight was going to lose the game on a call like that."

I'll tell you another officiating story. We were playing Alabama in the 1965 Orange Bowl. Alabama, throughout the season, had often used a tackle eligible pass play. If the end outside that tackle moves back a couple of steps, he becomes a flanker back and the tackle becomes the end — and thus eligible to catch a pass. To keep from having too many players in the backfield, the flanker on the other side of the field moves up on the line and becomes an end.

From ground level, where we coaches are standing — or from the position of the defensive backs — it was hard to tell whether that tackle was eligible or not. Often, nobody would be on him if he went out for a pass. Which is what made the play so effective.

In fact, during the regular season, the Southeastern officials had trouble with it, so they had devised a set of signals among themselves. The head linesman, who was looking down the line of scrimmage, would give a little hand signal to the deep officials if the tackle was eligible so there wouldn't be any mixup.

When the split crew went over things before the game, the head of the Big Eight officials told the SEC guys, "You shouldn't give any kind of signal as to what kind of a play is coming up. That's not a part of officiating."

I found out about it and told the Big Eight guy, "Hell, whose side are you on? Just tell us the hand signal so we'll

That's one of those times I didn't agree with the ref.

know how to defense them." But he didn't. He just told me, "That's not a part of officiating." We never did know the hand signal — if they did use it — and half the time we never could figure out whether the tackle was eligible or not. And the guy caught those tackle eligible passes like mad against us all night. That was one time when our own official screwed us up. The tackle was a former fullback named Duncan. I see Duncan occasionaly. He still kids me about it.

Another good officiating story happened in that 1969 Southern Cal game in Lincoln. USC was penalized four times in the first half for pass interference and even though he was ahead, John McKay was livid. He was muttering to himself when we headed for the dressing rooms. Suddenly, I found myself walking next to him. I couldn't help but grin. "Well, John," I said, "how do you like my brother's officiating?"

Then there was the time at the end of the 1971 season. We had beaten Oklahoma in that "Game of the Century" to go 11-0. Before we played Alabama in the Orange Bowl for the national championship, we went over to Hawaii.

We had nothing to gain and everything to lose by playing that game. But we didn't feel Hawaii was going to be a big threat to us. They didn't have that good a team. So, we didn't really clamp down on our players very much. We had some nights where we took a bed check on them — like the night before the game — but the rest of the time we weren't very strict.

Naturally, we were highly favored. But, I got a little worried as game time approached. I had been warned about the island officials. They used the same bunch of refs for all the games over there. And, of course, they were never going to see you again, so you didn't have a whole lot of recourse if they favored the home team.

But I had been to Hawaii for the Hula Bowl game several times. And I had gotten to know the guy who was the referee for all the big games over there. His name was Earl Galdiera. He was going to be working our game.

I'd hang my head too after a call like that!

Earl came up to me before the game and wanted to know if I would hire him to be one of the officials when Hawaii played a return game in Lincoln, which was scheduled for 1978. I told him I'd try to arrange it. Incidentally, he did come over, and he worked a good game.

But over there in '71, even though we were favored to run away with it, Hawaii scored first on us early in the first half. They kicked a field goal and were ahead, 3-0. Even at halftime it was still reasonably close. And we had gotten a couple of real lousy calls against us during the first half.

Before going into the dressing room at halftime, I got him over to the sidelines and said, "Earl, I can't bring you over to Lincoln for the return game if you're going to work a game like this."

I think as soon as the second half started a flag was thrown on Hawaii before they ever snapped the ball. And everything was alright from there on in. Actually, I think I had a right to be disturbed with the officiating in the first half. I thought they were trying to build things up for a big upset. Actually, as it worked out, we won rather handily, 45-3. But I didn't feel we were out of the woods at halftime.

Of course we followed that with a great game and almost as lopsided a victory, 38-6, against Alabama in the Orange Bowl to finish with a perfect 13-0 record and our second straight national championship.

I've never been able to get real mad at the officials, because I was one myself when I was coaching at the high school level. Jim Ross and I would work games together.

I'll never forget the game one night in the town of Onoway, Michigan. We forgot our stop watch. We didn't know what to do, but we found a tire guage. It looked like a stop watch. We'd keep looking at the tire guage like it was the official time. We were really just guessing the best we could by our wrist watch.

Then there was the time I needed to borrow a pair of ref's pants. I knew Jim had an extra pair. But the son of a gun sewed 'em up on me, so I couldn't get them around my waist. I was having a hell of a time. He started to laugh. He showed me how he had sewed the seams up so I couldn't get into them. We had some great times in our officiating days.

We often went over to officiate basketball games in Petoskey. Mike Corgan was coaching over there. He was the assistant basketball coach and head football coach. After the games we used to have a few beers with Mike. It was after one of those sessions we rolled our car over.

Jim and I used to siphon gas out of the school bus for our cars. Otherwise we couldn't afford to make the trip. We only got paid $12.50 each to officiate.

chapter twenty-six

*Of the offers I had
The Los Angeles Rams job
was probably the most attractive*

Several times, during my years as the coach at Nebraska, I had contacts with other colleges about leaving to become the coach someplace else. The only college I actually visited, with the thought in mind that I might go there, was the University of Miami.

That was in 1965. We were down there for an Orange Bowl game. I did talk to them. But I was aware of some of the problems they had — especially the financial ones — and I was also aware that with the Dolphins coming in to Miami, those problems would multiply. Which they did. So, even though I liked the area, it was probably a good thing that I decided not to go there.

I remember one of the quotes I gave out for a reason for not taking the job at Miami. I told the press down there that I couldn't make a switch because my wife had just bought a new set of snow tires for her car. Anyway, I already had one of the best college coaching jobs in the country.

Several times I've been asked to rate the best college jobs. You'd have to list Notre Dame at or near the top. Notre Dame has universal recruiting appeal. Any good Catholic kid anywhere in the country, when he's growing up, has the dream of playing for the Irish. Notre Dame has alumni and fan support from all over the country. That has to be a big plus when it comes to recruiting. Some people say it is impossible to screw up at Notre Dame, but some have done it. Hugh Devore was there for just a short period of time. Back after Rockne, Hunk Anderson was also there just a short time. Then there was Terry Brennan. There may have been another one or two that the Irish were dissatisfied with. The thing is, screwing up at Notre Dame and screwing up at some other school is two different things. Screwing up at Notre Dame is losing three ball games. Screwing up at some other school may be losing six or seven.

The other "best jobs" change around through the years. Southern Cal has to be one of the best places for a college coach. They have great tradition in football. I think Penn State, over the years, has also been one of the best. Alabama is right up there too. And the University of Texas. And there is Oklahoma. And, in the last 20 years or so, Nebraska has joined that group.

But, when you get to the Nebraska situation, it's not as easy to recruit. I don't say that any coach just has a cakewalk. But Southern California has a density of population in that area. The high schools out there have year-round athletic programs. Also, compare the Nebraska situation to Penn State. They have solid control of all of eastern Pennsylvania. And they've got that big New York-New Jersey area right in their back yard. And being really the only major school in that eastern region, Penn State can control the recruiting in the area pretty well.

Texas belongs in the top group because Texas is THE university in a state where there are more quality high school football players than any other state in the country — with the possible exception of California. They not only play tremendously good high school football in Texas but they're one of the few states that allows spring ball at the high school level.

I believe Nebraska is on the fringe of those other schools, only because of the amount of effort a Nebraska coach must put into recruiting in order to be successful. We're not in a top area when it comes to recruiting. Oklahoma stays up there, partly on their reputation and partly because of their proximity to the State of Texas. The Sooners also have a large number of alumni in the Texas area. And they are wealthy alumni.

I overlooked one. Ohio State is in that same class. I can't put Michigan up there with those others, however. Michigan has to scramble a little. They've got Michigan State right in the same area. And they have to fight for kids with a lot of nearby schools — including Notre Dame. Michigan's recruiting is not on the same level as Ohio State. Like Texas, Ohio State is THE university in their state.

Michigan has done a fine job since Schembechler became the coach. But that's a lot like our situation at Nebraska. In the last 20 years both schools have done well. But that's because the coaching staffs were willing to work like heck. That was not always the case.

If you want to expand the list, then you would add Pittsburgh and Arkansas.

We stayed up with the Joneses, so to speak, because of the tremendous dedication of the coaching staff. It's probably more competitive now than it was when I was coaching. It does seem, however, that a few years ago there were more schools in the Big Eight getting more good kids. I think it was when the 45 scholarship rule was in effect. We could take 45, but the Big Ten schools could only take 30. That's when we made some real inroads nationally as a conference.

In recent years, some of the schools in the Big Eight are feeling the pinch when it comes to getting the really top players. With more scholarships allowed, they were able to do better.

Phyllis and I returning from a trip in 1963.

To get back to job offers I had, in addition to the calls I had from several colleges, I had various contacts with pro teams while I was coaching at Nebraska.

I was approached by the Los Angeles Rams. It was the one job which to me was the most attractive. I wished I had more time to consider the offer. But they contacted me when we were getting ready for an Orange bowl game. It was 1965. It was the year they let George Allen go the first time — the year they eventually hired Tommy Prothro. I didn't go out there for a visit with them as they wanted. I felt I owed my loyalty to Nebraska and the team — to get them as ready as possible for the bowl game. The people with the Rams wanted to do something right then. I thought if they were interested that much in me they would wait until the bowl game was over. But they didn't. So they hired Prothro, who was right there in L.A. coaching UCLA.

One other time I talked with one of the Rooneys in Pittsburgh. That was before the Steelers had their new stadium. He asked me if I was interested and I told him no.

I also talked to Phipps one time, the owner of the Denver Broncos. It was over at Charlie Thone's house. That was serious to some degree. That was in the late 60s.

Then, a year or two later, when Lou Saban quit the job at Denver, he called me and asked me if I was interested. And I said, "Lou, should I be?" And he said, "No, I don't think so." And that was the end of that. At that time they had not built their new stadium and the Broncos were not the same caliber team they were later on.

The last chance I had was the year I quit coaching at Nebraska and turned things over to Tom — following the 1972 season. Billy Sullivan, the owner of the New England Patriots and I sat down and talked. I went out and visited their facilities. I was quite close on that one. There were several members of our coaching staff who were willing to go. And several of them who weren't. I had even gone so far as to line up some coaches for those other spots. I had talked with Bill Austin, who had been a former head coach in the pros. I also talked to Dick Nolan, who was the head coach for a couple of different NFL teams. I talked to various people to see who I would get as a staff.

Monte Kiffin was all for going. He was gung ho. And my wife thought I was going to go. In fact, I had to place a call from my house to Billy Sullivan. I had stalled around long enough. And Phyllis thought I was going to tell him I was taking the job. And I think Monte did. Monte was right there. But I told Sullivan I just didn't want to coach anymore. If I had wanted to coach some more, I would have stayed on at Nebraska.

I was very seriously thinking about the New England job, however. I had gone out there and looked over their facility. But a lot of improvement was needed — improvements which were later made. Their players, at that time, when they went out for practice — at a field some distance from their dressing rooms — had to carry a sack lunch. They needed to get a lot of things going there.

But Billy Sullivan is a very, very fine person. Even after I told him no, he sent Phyllis and me a really nice set of crystal glasses. A quite expensive set. He sent them just as a present.

When I decided against the job, I recommended Chuck Fairbanks to Billy. I don't know how much weight my recommendation carried, but I told him, "Here is a guy who just finished beating us for the Big Eight championship. I've known Chuck for a long while. I think he's a fine coach." And so Chuck talked to Billy and was hired.

I don't think I was the first choice on Billy Sullivan's list. I think he first talked to Joe Paterno. And then I think he might have talked to me second. And then Chuck.

I think I could have had the Rams job if I'd shown more interest. I don't know about Pittsburgh. We were in a very preliminary stage in those discussions. They hired Bill Austin that year. Then they later fired him. But Pittsburgh did not have the facilities they have now. When I talked to Pittsburgh and Denver, they didn't have the facilities. If they had, those jobs would have been a lot more attractive.

There would be a lot of difference between coaching college and pro ball. And I think the difference gets greater every year, because of the lack of control a pro coach really has over his players. That's mostly caused by the money thing. In some instances you have a coach who is working for maybe $300,000 a year less than some player he is trying to coach. It's the same thing in pro baseball. Hell, managers have problems with what they want the guy to do and what he'll do. The same thing applies in pro football.

I don't say that guys aren't guys. And there are certain coaches, like Tom Landry at Dallas, who have the respect of their players — regardless of how much they are making. I think Don Shula at Miami has the respect of his players. And there are others. Chuck Knox, Don Coryell, Dick Vermeil, and Bud Grant to mention a few. But there are not too many who have that real control. I would have hoped, had I decided to stay in coaching and gone with a pro team, that I would have been able to hold somewhat that same kind of control over a team that a person like Landry or Shula does.

But I never was built to be quite as standoffish as Landry, perhaps. And I think with a certain amount of standoffishness there is a little awe that is built up among the players. If they don't feel like they can get to you real quick personally, a little awe is built up. And I think maybe that's pretty good.

I think the salary differences between a coach and the players, when I thought of getting involved in pro football, was not as great as it is now. I think the players today would be harder to deal with than they were 10-15 years ago. To me, a pro job today in any sport, I don't care, basketball, football, hockey, anything, is a real precarious way of making a living. There are some guys doing it — and making some good money — but I don't envy them a bit.

Speaking of being recruited away from the Nebraska coaching job, there were rumors from time to time that I was being recruited to run for political office. I had people

Here I am explaining to Arnold Palmer how to correct his slice.

ask me if I were interested, but there was never anything serious that came from those discussions. I have always been very plain and simple in telling people that I was not interested in politics in any way, shape or form. I don't want to get involved. I think you are less your own person when you're involved in politics than any possible occupation.

Regarding my only experience of helping somebody in politics, I like to tell the story about when Jim Ross and I were out campaigning for Ole Olson for county commissioner when Jim and I were high school coaches in Michigan.

We knocked on this one farmer's door and asked him to vote for Ole. The farmer said, "You mean the Ole Olson who used to be the tender at the drawbridge?" And we said, "Yep, that's the gentleman."

"Well," the farmer said, "Come in and let me tell you about that Ole Olson. When he was working on that drawbridge, I had a very fine bull. He kept my cows very happy. But the bull got sick one time and I called the vet. The vet said, 'There's nothing wrong with the bull except he's constipated. I'm going to give you a recipe for a solution. You mix it up in a pail. Then, insert a funnel in the bull's rectum. Pour the solution in and he'll be fine again in no time.'

"Well," the farmer continued, "I got the solution all mixed up just like he told me. Then I started looking around for a funnel, but I couldn't find one. Then I looked over in the corner of the barn and I spotted my boy's bugle. So I took the bugle and inserted the small end in the bull's rectum. And I took the pail with the solution in it, and poured the solution in the big end of the bugle.

"I had almost all the solution poured in when the 4:10 train went by and startled the bull. That bull busted out of his stall. He busts out of the barn. And he heads down the road toward the drawbridge where Ole Olson is the drawbridge tender. That bull is a tootin' and a fartin' — and a tootin' and a fartin'. And that Ole Olson, he opens up the drawbridge.

"The bull falls in the river and drowns. Now you two guys want me to vote for some dumb sonofagun who can't tell a bull with a bugle in his ass from a tug boat?"

Seriously, I did get involved in one political campaign. I tried to help Paul Douglas the time when he first ran for State Attorney General.

I took Paul around a few places. Sort of a mini campaign. When we had these golf stags and things like that I would introduce him. I don't think many people resented it. I think most of the people connected with the university liked Paul.

But then I wrote a couple of letters to people, asking for their support, on university stationery.

Now you remember Dick Davis. He was one of the better players I coached at Nebraska. Well, Dick's dad was employed by Frank Morrison, Paul's opponent. I don't know whether Dick talked to his dad about needing some help for Paul Douglas or what. I know that Paul and I went up to Omaha and met with two black doctors and Charles Washington. We met with them, trying to solicit some help from the black community. But I did write those letters. And of course Morrison got wind of it. And he was really all over the university and me for using the school stationery and the school's secretary to work politically. That ended my political career — in a hurry!

chapter twenty-seven

*Good, loyal assistants
are the key to success
for every head coach*

Although we had a lot of fun while coaching the College-Pro All-Star Game, it was also hard work. We were in Chicago the better part of a month, and there was one bad thing that came from the experience. I think our taking part in that all-star game hurt us for my final season at Nebraska. I think it hampered our getting properly prepared, particularly for our 1972 opener at UCLA.

We were mentally tired of coaching football when we returned from Chicago. Had we come back to Lincoln and gone right to work — full steam — we wouldn't have been hurt in our own preparations for UCLA, but everybody got back and relaxed for awhile. We just started getting ready a little later than we should have.

As a result, when the Bruins kicked a field goal in the closing seconds of the game to beat us, 20-17, it marked the first game we had lost since the fourth game of the 1969 season.

One of our other problems in that game was that I probably underestimated UCLA. They had not had a very good season the year before, and we had seen some film on them and were not all that impressed. But we didn't realize what kind of a back Wendell Tyler was, nor did we know how good some of those other people they had were. They were all fine football players.

There was also one other factor we hadn't taken into account. Doug Weaver. Weaver was the defensive coach for Pepper Rodgers, and he always defensed Nebraska very well.

He was the defensive coordinator for Kansas when they beat us two years in a row, in 1967 and '68, and also the next year, when we were lucky enough to come from behind to win at the end of the game with the aid of a pass interference call. That was the game which started our long winning streak. Then there we were in Los Angeles, playing a Pepper Rodgers-coached team again — with Weaver preparing their defense again — in what turned out to be the game which ended the streak.

We had one heckuva time moving the ball against Kansas when Doug was preparing their defense. At that time, we were using a lot of Michigan State stuff, and Weaver grew up at Michigan State. He played there. He is a very, very intelligent person. Doug Weaver, I felt, always seemed to anticipate more what we were going to do than any defensive coordinator we played against. Doug is now the athletic director at Michigan State.

For some reason, even though he was a great defensive assistant, Doug never did much as a head coach at either Kansas State or Southern Illinois. But I think Doug is a real sharp guy. I always had a high regard for him.

He was probably just in bad situations — in the wrong place at the wrong time — when he had his chances as a head coach, but he was a great assistant.

Good assistant coaches are the real key to the success of any head coach. The assistants with whom I was associated, both as a fellow assistant at Michigan State and as a head coach at Wyoming and Nebraska, were tremendously important to the program. If there is one thing I was able to do well during my coaching career, it was picking people who were good assistant coaches.

Lloyd Eaton, who was with me at Wyoming, is a good example. He was a fine coach. So was Jim Ross, who has been with me for a long time. Not only was Jim a fine coach in his own right, but he has a great many other talents. Guys like Mike Corgan, with his enthusiasm, and George Kelly, Carl Selmer, with his good football brain, and certainly Tom Osborne, who has done a superb job since taking over at Nebraska . . . those people were all fine assistants. So was John Melton, who is a sharp guy and still a good coach. With his sense of humor, John keeps things in balance. He's also been one of our best recruiters over the years. Another great recruiter and a fine line coach is Clete Fischer. Assistant coaches like Monte Kiffin, Warren Powers, Bill Thornton and Jim Walden are among others who deserve special mention.

That's the thing that has been real, real important. The assistants do the work. I think a tremendous amount of the credit should be given to them, and to the many others who have worked with us over the years, like Don Bryant in the promotion of our program as the sports information director. We had Wiles Hallock in that same job at Wyoming. He's now the commissioner of the Pac-10 Conference.

There are lots of other people with whom I have been closely associated, like our trainers Paul Schneider and George Sullivan. It's so important to have loyal people on the staff, especially if they are people who are in contact with your players, like the trainers, for instance, or the equipment manager. You certainly wouldn't want an equipment manager who is not the right kind of a guy. He's in contact with the players every day, and he can do a lot to help keep them happy — or make them surly and hard to get along with.

The No. 1 thing you need in a staff is loyalty. The next thing is an ability to do the job.

The same thing applies for me now as athletic director. I've got some great coaches, and they're doing a good job. I was with two coaches who were regarded as great coaches — Biggie Munn and Duffy Daugherty — and they surrounded themselves with guys who proved they had a lot of ability. Bill Yeoman, now at Houston; Dan Devine; Lou Agase — who was a fine football coach; Doug Weaver; Buck Nystrom; the guy who went to Minnesota, Cal Stoll. Those were just some of the fellows who were on the staff at Michigan State when I was an assistant there.

To me, after seeing how Biggie and Duffy operated, it was obvious that the big key to getting things done was to have a great group of assistants.

I think the biggest mistake I made when I first went to Wyoming was trying to do all the coaching myself. Hell, I was trying to do everything. I think that led to a rather mediocre season. I didn't know better, or didn't have enough confidence, to turn enough over to the assistants. I think, perhaps, any head coach coming into a job for the first year, is going to make that mistake by trying to do too much of the coaching.

The more credit and responsibility an assistant coach is given, the better job he'll do. If he knows he's really in charge of the players at the position he's coaching, he's going to take a lot more pride in what he does.

I'm reminded of when I first went to Michigan State and was put in charge of the defensive backs and our pass defense. I didn't know anything about a sophisticated pass defense, coming out of the high school ranks as I had, but I tried to learn all I could. I got hold of Howard Brinker of the Cleveland Browns staff. I sat down with him and we talked. He was very kind and helpful to me. Then I watched film for hours. And what happened? Michigan State went from last in the Big Ten to the top. We became the best team against the pass in the league.

The same thing happened here at Nebraska. We have stayed, over the years, at or near the top in the nation in several statistical categories. That indicates good kids, but it also indicates good assistant coaches.

You're really a dummy if you think you've done it all as the head coach, or, if you think, while you're doing it, that you can do it all.

The need to surround myself with good people is the same now that I am the athletic director on a full-time basis. When I first became athletic director, and was coaching too, there really wasn't the impact of being athletic director. Jim Ross quit coaching at the varsity level in order to do a lot of the athletic director's work. Don Bryant also has been a great help as assistant athletic director. And Jim Pittenger was also a great help to me. He ran the entire ticket operation without much supervision, and he did a great job. Now, Helen Ruth Wagner, under difficult situations, does the best job of any ticket manager in our conference. A lot of the departments pretty much run themselves.

When I quit coaching, it was a gradual change for me to take the proper interest in all sports, and it was difficult for me to just sit in the office.

But I know the regents want a successful program, and they want it operated within the budget. Getting good people has again been the key, and I think we've got them. Some of them I didn't pick. Some of them I did.

Frank Sevigne was here when I arrived, but Francis Allen, Cal Bentz, Bob Fehrs, John Sanders and Moe Iba represent some of the changes I've made, and I think they-'re all doing a good job.

Larry Romjue is a good golf coach, and young Kerry McDermott will do a good job with tennis.

We have had the best all-around athletic program in the Big Eight Conference the last two years.

Also, in the past seven years, Nebraska has developed one of the best women's athletic programs in the country. We have a fine director of athletics in Dr. June Davis, and she has surrounded herself with some good people.

No one can question John Melton's coaching ability.
But, his taste in hats is another thing.

It's been a challenging job to worry about the success of every sport — not just about football. I've enjoyed and appreciated Nebraska and really feel like it's home. The job of a coach's wife and family is even tougher than that faced by the coach. I really appreciate the understanding and support of my wife, Phyllis, and our children, Patricia and Mike.